YOUNG, MUSLIM AND

Experiences, identi
pathways into crime

Mohammed Qasim

C000091430

P

First published in Great Britain in 2018 by

Policy Press
University of Bristol
1-9 Old Park Hill
Bristol
BS2 8BB
UK
t: +44 (0)117 954 5940
pp-info@bristol.ac.uk
www.policypress.co.uk

North America office:
Policy Press
c/o The University of Chicago Press
1427 East 60th Street
Chicago, IL 60637, USA
t: +1 773 702 7700
f: +1 773-702-9756
sales@press.uchicago.edu
www.press.uchicago.edu

© Policy Press 2018

British Library Cataloguing in Publication Data
A catalogue record for this book is available from the British Library

Library of Congress Cataloging-in-Publication Data
A catalog record for this book has been requested

ISBN 978-1-4473-4150-5 paperback
ISBN 978-1-4473-4148-2 hardcover
ISBN 978-1-4473-4151-2 ePub
ISBN 978-1-4473-4152-9 Mobi
ISBN 978-1-4473-4149-9 ePdf

The right of Mohammed Qasim to be identified as author of this work has been asserted by him in accordance with the Copyright, Designs and Patents Act 1988.

All rights reserved: no part of this publication may be reproduced, stored in a retrieval system, or transmitted in any form or by any means, electronic, mechanical, photocopying, recording, or otherwise without the prior permission of Policy Press.

The statements and opinions contained within this publication are solely those of the author and not of the University of Bristol or Policy Press. The University of Bristol and Policy Press disclaim responsibility for any injury to persons or property resulting from any material published in this publication.

Policy Press works to counter discrimination on grounds of gender, race, disability, age and sexuality.

Cover design by Andrew Corbett
Front cover image: Getty
Printed and bound in Great Britain by CMP, Poole
Policy Press uses environmentally responsible print partners

This book is dedicated to the early Pakistani migrants who arrived in the UK; those individuals who, like my grandfather, are sadly no longer with us. We are forever grateful for the sacrifices they made and are incredibly appreciative of their hard work. We pray that God blesses them for the opportunities they left us with.

Contents

Glossary

7/7	the London bombings of 2005
9/11	attacks on the US in 2001, including the World Trade Center
apnania	Pakistani girls
apnas	Pakistanis, your own people
apni zabaan	mother tongue
Aslaam Alaikum	peace be with you
Azaan	call to prayer
banda	people
bare	a lot of
bare coin	a lot of money
baseti	insulting
bender	a binge, a night out, getting drunk or high
bhai	brother
block	segregation (in prison)
blud	bro, blood brother
BME	Black and Minority Ethnic
bud	cannabis
burn	cigarettes
canteen	weekly shopping, which includes belongings
chacha	term of respect to address a male elder, uncle
chatting it	speaking nonsense
chesa	drugs
chill	spend time, hang out
chip	run away
contact	drug dealer
danna	ounce
Dawah	preaching about Islam
Deen	Islamic way
digits	phone number
dobra	good
down block	segregated
down with, to be	allies
dps	drug deal drop-offs
Duniya	the world
Emaan	faith
Fajr	sunrise prayer
Five-O	police
fuck someone up	beat someone up

game, the	drug dealing
get busted	be caught by the police
gora(s)	white person (people)
goree	white female
halal	meat Muslims are allowed to eat
haraam	forbidden under Islamic law, meat Muslims must not eat
hefty sentence	long prison sentence
hench	physically large and impressive
hijab	headscarf
hustling	selling drugs
Imam	priest, leader of prayers, teacher of religion
inside	in prison
Itikaaf	spending the last ten days of Ramadan in seclusion
Izzat	respect, honour
joint	cannabis cigarette
Jumma	Friday prayers
jumped	attacked in a fight
junkies	drug addicts
Kala	black man
Kasam se	honestly
kasmay	honestly
KoKa	cocaine
Koti	large house
lamp	punch
link (n.)	drug dealer
link (v.)	meet
locked up	imprisoned
maal	used for any illegal drugs, but mostly used to refer to heroin
mangies	people newly arrived from Pakistan
mans	friends
masjid	place of worship
mawe	police
muppet	idiot
namaza	the five daily prayers of Islam
next mans	middlemen, drug dealers
nonce	rapist
on tag	released from prison but wearing an electronic tracking device on the ankle
on tick	on credit

outside charge	new criminal charge
owt	anything
pad (in jail)	cell
paper	money
peeps	people
petrol legger	driving off without paying for fuel at a petrol station
Pothwari	a Pakistani dialect
Purees	paying respects to those who have lost a relative
puria (pl. *puraih*)	small bag of heroin
quna	sins
raise	profit, money
Ramadan	month of fasting
rep	reputation, credibility
ripps	robbing/stealing
round, a	selling and delivering drugs
saada	simple, unintelligent
Salah	prayer
score	buy drugs
screw	prison officer
Sharaab	alcohol
shisha lounge	a place to smoke a hookah, shisha being the tobacco used
shotter	drug dealer
sick	nice
sick killing	a lot of money
sick paper	a lot of money
skunk	skunkweed, a potent variety of cannabis
slammed	punished harshly
smack-heads	drug addicts
smash (a woman)	have sex with
smashing it	making a lot of money illegally
smoke	cannabis, to smoke cannabis
snitch	police informer
spice	a substitute for cannabis that gives a high but is not detectable in drugs tests
stinker	ugly woman
straight	honest, crime free
stretch	prison sentence
summat	something
taxed	stole
tinkle	phone call

twat	idiot
yaar	mate, friend
Zikr	Islamic meditation

Acknowledgements

No study can be completed without the support and guidance of others and that is certainly true in the case of this book. I would like to thank a number of individuals whose support has been greatly valued, beginning by thanking my mother and my father. Thanks to my brothers Tariq, Khalid and Shahid who have encouraged me to continue with my research. Thanks to my wife Zalekha who has had the patience to put up with me disappearing for much of the day to complete this book. I dedicate this book to my sons Musa and Ebraheem, as well as my nephew Abu Bakr and my niece Aminah.

My thanks also go out to friends, Colin, Julie, Ayaz, Ramzan, Arshad and Abdul who have been incredibly supportive in their advice and encouragement. With great appreciation I acknowledge my colleagues at Gower College Swansea, particularly Ceri Low and Chris Williams.

I am grateful to Professor Kevin Haines, Professor Stephen Case, who gave me invaluable advice throughout my field work, and Professor Colin Webster who guided me through every stage of writing this book.

Finally, this work owes great gratitude to the young men whose lives were studied, young men who have left me feeling honoured and privileged that they trusted me in undertaking the task of studying their lives. I could not thank these young men enough and hope that this work does justice to their lives.

Introduction

"I'm young, I'm a Muslim and I'm also a criminal, who the fuck's gonna give me a job?" yelled Ahmed one evening as we stood on the street corner, not far from where he lived. We had been discussing the prospect of him finding a legal job and turning away from a life of crime. But Ahmed was clearly furious at the thought of going 'straight'; he felt there were few other ways in which to make money than to be involved with the sale of illegal drugs. Ahmed had been hustling [selling drugs] for the past six years and despite having served a number of custodial sentences for violence and drug-related crimes, he continued to sell drugs.

While there were jobs in Bradford, I had to remind myself that there was potentially a lot of truth in what Ahmed was telling me. Why would anyone want to employ him? What could he offer an employer? Despite being a bubbly character and someone who seemed to be incredibly shrewd for the street life, Ahmed had no formal qualifications: he left school without any GCSEs and had no previous job experience other than the time when he worked at his uncle's takeaway when he was 15. I also had to consider that jobs were difficult to come by in Bradford today, particularly for those individuals, like Ahmed, who had extensive criminal records and were from ethnic minority backgrounds. The title of this book derives from what Ahmed explained to me on that particular evening, telling me that he was 'young, Muslim and criminal'. It was precisely this experience that I wanted to learn more about, I wanted to find out why young men like Ahmed became involved with drugs and turned to selling them rather than taking alternative paths. I was driven to try and understand why young men who were British born and spoke English fluently would struggle to find work.

In order to gain a true insight into the lives and behaviours of young British Muslim men who offend, I was aware that I would have to interact in as many ways as possible with them. This involved speaking with them, observing them in their natural setting and conducting in-depth interviews with them. Adler (1993: 28) on this point insists, 'I feel strongly that to ensure accuracy, research on deviant groups must be conducted in the settings where it naturally occurs'. The young British Pakistani Muslim men in this study have experienced life in raw terms, where they sense the factors involved rather than being able to analyse their experience in terms of academic theory. This book therefore seeks to combine both perspectives, permitting the often inchoate articulation of barely understood feelings, and a context in which to locate such experience. In that sense, with regard to young men getting into trouble it is important to highlight that there is passion in their lives that does not always easily come through in other academic studies of them and which I try to capture in this book.

Aim of the book

The timing of this book could not be more significant as it comes during a period when there is increasing speculation that the British Muslim individual is 'suspicious' (Pantazis and Pemberton, 2009) and regarded by many to be an 'enemy within' (Hudson, 2007). British Muslim individuals are today portrayed as closely associated with a range of criminal behaviour, particularly with crimes such as terrorism (Hargreaves, 2014), violence, sexual abuse, drugs (Pring, 1996; Trivedi, 1997; Hopkins Burke, 1999; Barn, 2011; Gill and Harrison, 2015; Qasim, 2017), urban unrest and street crime (Mythen et al, 2009). However, what is interesting to learn is that despite increasing speculation around their offending behaviours, little attention has so far been given to the views of those on the inside (M.Y. Alam, 2006; Chakraborti, 2007; Hargreaves, 2014). Archer (2003) highlights that in contrast to the sensationalised and negative stereotypical representations of Muslim masculinity, relatively little work has attempted to address young British Muslim men's own views and experiences. Similarly, Mythen and colleagues (2009: 740) argue that 'it would not be stretching the truth to state that young Muslims have been talked at, talked for and talked around. They have not been talked to'. This, as some commentators have previously highlighted, has left a gap in contemporary British criminological academic contributions to the understanding of the qualitative experiences of young Muslim men and crime (Quraishi, 2005; Bolognani, 2009; Qasim, 2017).

This book consequently aims to offer an insight into the lives of a social group of British-born Pakistani Muslim men (also known as The Boys) who were involved in a range of offending behaviours. The Boys lived in a tight-knit Pakistani community in Bradford, England, and this book aims to understand their lives, taking into account their socioeconomic situation, the make-up of their community, the cultural and religious influences which impacted on them and on their lives and their involvement in crime. This book attempts to understand why The Boys were involved in crime and what factors, if any, motivated them to offend, exploring whether there were other possible and unique explanations for their offending such as, for example, cultural or religious factors.

While the aim of this book is to understand the lives and behaviours of a social group of young British-born Pakistani Muslim men who offend, it is important to point out from the very outset that it does not intend to deliberately discriminate against the individuals concerned by painting them in a negative manner. Nor does it aim to be over-sympathetic to why they offend. Instead this book aims to understand the lives and behaviours of the men from a non-biased viewpoint, being aware that the role of the researcher should be as neutral as possible in order for his or her findings to be unbiased or influenced.

Conducting the research

One of the key challenges when studying the lives of offenders is making contact and in this section I discuss how I made contact with The Boys.

It was while living in Bradford, some 12 years ago that I knew a number of young British Pakistani Muslim men who carried a reputation within the neighbourhood as troublemakers. These young men were a close-knit group of friends who had grown up together living in the same neighbourhood. They were rambunctious, loud and boisterous, routinely seen hanging around on street corners, particularly by the corner shop (referred to as Zaks and which was a popular haunt[1]). They were not new to trouble, with many of the local residents having witnessed them and their regular encounters with the police. There was one particular occasion when I saw some of The Boys arrested on the street corners, and another when police turned up at one of their houses. On seeing the police, the individual in question had run away, only to be arrested by several police officers further down the road, handcuffed and walked back to their car.

I consequently decided, based on the purpose of the research, to conduct my study on the lives of this particular group of young men. However, I was attentive to a number of challenges that were present. The foremost of these challenges was that I had not seen or spoken with the young men for a considerable number of years, which raised the question as to whether they were still living in the same neighbourhood. After numerous phone calls to individuals who I knew lived in the same area as The Boys, it was established that, with a few exceptions, most of the young men continued to reside in the same locality. More importantly, I learned that they continued to belong to the same social group as they did when I last lived in the vicinity. The difference was that, whereas previously the young men would socialise on street corners, socialising these days was done predominantly in either their cars or at one of their flats. What's more, I learned that, just as The Boys would once gather on the street corners and by Zaks, today there was a new generation of youth made up of younger boys who, within their own social group, would hang around on the exact same street corners as The Boys used to. This group of younger boys were referred to by the older boys as The Kids (they were predominantly in their late teens, with one or two in their early twenties). Consequently, I was also faced with the curious possibility that the target group, The Boys, were (at the time of his research) gradually becoming an older generation and being displaced or at least supplemented by a younger generation. This had methodological significance as it meant that the research made sense of those boys at that time and in that place with the possibility (and indeed probability) that their experience could safely be generalised to other young men of identical age but in various multiple locations. However, through the research it was likely to show that what was true of the target population could not be guaranteed to be true of the upcoming younger generation. Even though the younger generation shared similar experiences and outlooks, these were not certain to replicate in their entirety those of the older boys in this study.

Making contact with The Boys

I considered that the best way to encourage The Boys to participate in the study was initially to approach individuals who I knew better than the others. The reasoning behind this was that once these young men agreed to participate, I could then rely on them to help persuade the others to also join the study. This was a variation of the snowball effect – gaining access to other, relatively junior status group members through being accepted by what Holloway (1997) and Greig and Taylor (1999) call gatekeepers. On this point, Fetterman (1998: 34) in his work on ethnography states that 'in many instances access is clearly impossible, without some escort'.

Two of The Boys whom I knew better than the others, having once played cricket and football with them, were Kamran and Salman.[2] One evening, with the help of a friend (a relative of Kamran), I arranged to meet Kamran and Salman at a local cafe. Both appeared genuinely pleased to see me and spoke of how they had not seen me for a good number of years. I then moved on to ask if they would allow me to study their lives. At first both appeared somewhat troubled with the idea. Kamran was particularly fearful that by taking part in the study he may expose his criminal activities, and was concerned about how information obtained about him would be used. It is well known that those involved in crime are cautious about allowing anyone to study their lives, aware that allowing this could potentially expose the types of crimes that they are involved in or are planning to commit (Taylor, 2009; Abrams, 2015). But this also raises the questions, why would anyone want their lives to be examined so closely? And what is the benefit for them in doing so? As expected, the issue of confidentiality and anonymity were major concerns for the young men. Martin (2000), drawing on her work in prison settings, argues that confidentiality should never be taken lightly by researchers when conducting research on those who offend, and I had to address these issues very seriously. After reassuring Kamran and Salman that the study would be kept entirely confidential, and that I would do them 'no dirt' with what was discovered about them, they agreed to participate. They even agreed to help encourage some of the other young men who were part of their social group to take part in the study.

A few days later, I met with other members of the target group at one of their flats to discuss the study. After informing them about the study and what it would involve, I was surprised to see just how interested The Boys were in me, questioning me as to where I was currently living, where I was working and if I had any plans to move back to Bradford on a more permanent basis. I spoke at some length about my own life, aware, as Berk and Adams (1970) state, that by revealing intimate facts about themselves researchers increase the probability that they will be accepted by the group (as long as the intimacies do not reveal the observer as someone who cannot be trusted).

I had expected the proposed target population to be cautious of the study and to question why I wanted to conduct a detailed study of their lives, but I was pleasantly surprised to witness just how easy acceptance was by The Boys. One possible explanation was because they were aware that Kamran and Salman had already agreed to participate in the research, and felt that the study had been vetted. Another was because they already knew me and felt that they could trust me to bring them no harm.

The fieldwork process

The fieldwork for this research was conducted over a relatively lengthy period – as befits a phenomenological approach – from December 2010 to November 2014. Over this period, I spent a considerable time with the young men in their natural setting, aware, as Wolcott (1995) argues, that fieldwork is a process that assumes a degree of wholehearted commitment. During the first three years of the study

I spent significant time with The Boys, through whom I was later able to gain access to The Kids. The latter in many ways appeared to be replicating the lives of former, hanging out on the streets.

The fieldwork for this research was facilitated by two factors in particular: first, because prior to conducting the study I was acquainted with The Boys; and second, I had a number of commonalities with the study's participants. According to Bryman (2004), there are a number of characteristics that may affect the research of which the researcher needs to be aware, including age, gender, social background (or class) and education level. Accordingly, I had shared experiences with the young men whose lives I had chosen to study, having once lived not far from them. Other commonalities were being of a similar age, and having attended some of the same schools. Furthermore, I am of Pakistani ethnicity and of Muslim faith, and it was anticipated from the outset that these commonalities and factors would help with access and also help build rapport with the young Pakistani Muslim men. Berk and Adams (1970) point out that if there is a large gap in social background between the investigator and his or her subjects it can make establishing ongoing rapport an especially formidable task.

Reflexivity was significant to this study

While there have been several attempts to undertake research investigating why so many young British Pakistani Muslim men seem to get into trouble, most of these have been limited in their success. This is in no way a reflection on the skills of the researchers, many of whom have been gifted academics, but the core issue has been how the target population has perceived the researchers, the question-askers, the observers of their lives. If for any reason the target population has concerns or reservations then the best that will happen is that the data collected will be limited. In this case, since the target population was criminal and intensely wary of outsiders, the issue of reflexivity was a dominant methodological concern. Consequently, commonalities that I had with the target population helped to overcome barriers and gain insights into the lives of the young men. It is important to highlight that a researcher who was not known by the target population would have struggled to gain access and, more importantly, struggled to have understood the lives of the young men as they were lived. Although someone unknown to The Boys may have been treated with courtesy, there would nonetheless be risks of silent barriers. The degree of openness depended on the credibility of the person with whom The Boys were talking. If they found the person they were talking with to be acceptable then they were more likely to be open about themselves than if they had any reservations about the identity of the person asking questions or observing them.

There was also a risk that a non-Muslim researcher would have been perceived by The Boys as failing to understand from the outset the ways of thinking and behaviours that characterised their lives. This overlapped with ethnicity because although traditional ethnic culture and the universal religion of Islam are separate issues, there is considerable overlap. A non-Pakistani would have experienced the same difficulties with culture and tradition as a non-Muslim would have with Islam. Significantly, even a Muslim from an ethnic but non-Pakistani background would have experienced difficulties along these lines. This could mean that insights would be withheld, explanations not fully given and confidences not shared. The sense of the researcher being 'other' may dominate, no matter how well-liked the person might have been. For this reason it was anticipated that commonalities and prior knowledge with the study participants would make it easier to understand what The Boys meant when they spoke. According to Schutz (1962: 220), 'if two actors have prior knowledge of one another, then they are more likely to get their meaning across than if they do not know each other or each other's provinces of meaning'. Miner-Romanoff (2012: 14) also highlights that 'expert knowledge is invaluable in guiding interview questions, probing for participants' deeper meanings, and rendering the inquiry more meaningful'. This can also make communications elliptical at times because any group who know each other intimately often do not complete sentences in conversation, and can convey meaning with a word, a look or a gesture which is not spelled out, and is, therefore, not necessarily clear to the observer. Indeed, such communications can often be almost subconscious, for when people are so attuned to each other they know exactly what each other is conveying.[3]

Book overview

This book is split into seven chapters. Chapter One starts by discussing why young British-born Pakistani Muslim men are increasingly associated with crime and disorder today, paying close attention to some of the early incidents that led to these people being portrayed as more criminal. Given that very little previous research has examined criminological theories explaining offending by British Pakistani Muslim men, this chapter subsequently examines whether young British Pakistani Muslim men who offend do so for the same reasons as young people who offend in general or whether there are other possible and unique explanations for their offending such as, for example, religious or cultural elements. This chapter subsequently sets out the tone for the study by discussing how little is known as to why young British Pakistani Muslim men offend.

Chapter Two contextualises the research by taking an overview of the geographical location of where The Boys lived. It starts by examining the history of Bradford's textile trade, as the Pakistani migrants arrived in Bradford originally to work in the textile mills. However, due to the demise of the textile industry in the 1970s and 1980s, many of the city's migrants were left in a difficult financial situation. This chapter examines the challenges that the Pakistani migrants faced after the closure of the mills.

The young men in the study reside in an area of Bradford called Manningham, and this chapter examines the historical circumstances which contributed to the characteristics of this district. Also explored are the reasons why so many Pakistanis sought to live there even though the early Pakistani community faced a number of concerning issues when settling here, such as racism. However, while confronting racism is no longer a major concern for Manningham's Pakistani residents, there are other issues such as the growing fear of crime committed by young British Pakistani men and this chapter discusses these concerns.

Chapter Three investigates the identity, substructures and dynamics of the group of young men known as The Boys. A picture of the young men is presented by examining their personalities and traits in detail. This chapter is divided into sections that describe each of The Boys and which discuss aspects of their behaviours and personalities in more depth. This chapter moves on to discuss The Boys' time at school, examining how, for most of The Boys, offending started when they were still at school. As The Boys left their teen years behind, their offending gradually changed. From what was once regarded as petty crime, they moved onto more serious crime, their prime motivation for offending now being financial gain. This chapter examines the reasons behind this change.

As discussed in Chapter Three, many of the young men in the study sold illegal drugs and Chapter Four examines how they would go about their drug dealing. Selling drugs was a risky business, so in order to evade detection from the police The Boys had to be discreet. Drug dealing also involved shrewdness, the activity in many ways being similar to running a business. This meant buying drugs as cheaply as possible and then trying to sell them on to make maximum profit, and this chapter examines how The Boys would do so. The Boys consumed drugs, but a lot of the time what they used themselves differed from what they sold and this chapter examines why this was the case, asking why they did not want to consume the drugs that they sold. Many of the young men in the study also drank alcohol frequently with some of them drinking heavily and often. This chapter consequently examines the challenges that drinking alcohol presented in a neighbourhood where most of the residents were Muslims.

A theme that strongly emerged from observation and conversation with The Boys was their close relationship with prison. Chapter Five discusses this relationship, including consideration of their own experience of prison and its impact on them and their lives. A striking aspect of prison was how The Boys would become more devoted to Islamic faith while 'inside', and on their release would talk about Islam at some length. This chapter examines why this was the case, and what factors, if any, contributed to The Boys becoming more religious when they were in prison. On release, adjusting to outside life was at times exceptionally difficult, and the challenges they faced on their release are also examined in this chapter.

Chapter Six is split into two sections. The first half of the chapter focuses on the role that Pakistani culture played in the lives of The Boys while the second half explores the relationship they had with their Islamic faith. It is important to explore these influences because Pakistanis living in the UK bear complex identities, with a strong cultural and Islamic heritage (Werbner, 2004). It has been noted by some commentators that multiple sets of values cause second- and third-generation Pakistanis to suffer an 'identity conflict' (Archer, 2001; Cressey, 2002) and for this reason these were necessary to explore. Chapter Six consequently explores some of the challenges The Boys found with certain aspects of Pakistani culture. It then moves on to uncover their thoughts and experiences of Pakistan, a place which they would refer to frequently as 'back home', a country which all had visited during some stage of their lives.

The Boys considered their Islamic faith to be incredibly important, and this seemed odd at first glance given that they were troublesome delinquents who drank alcohol, slept around with girls and were involved with the consumption and sale of drugs. It is precisely the tension between all these aspects of their relationship with faith that made it interesting to study The Boys' perception of Islam and what role if any Islam played in their lives and in their thinking, or even in their offending.

Through a phenomenological study, a number of themes emerged which have been presented in this work. The conclusions and findings of this study are discussed in Chapter Seven. Chapter Seven starts by discussing how many of the young men's situations changed over the course of the study, and in some cases changed considerably, with some of The Boys now showing signs of desistance. Although they continued to hang out with one another, towards the latter part of the study some were doing so less frequently. This was almost certainly because of certain life-cycle events, such as getting married or starting a family, which impacted significantly on their outlook on life and which was now seeing behaviours slowly changing.

Notes

[1] The real names of the shops where The Boys socialised have been anonymised and they are instead referred to as Zaks.

[2] For anonymity reasons the names of The Boys have been changed.

[3] Given that I had been immersed in such prior knowledge and was pre-attuned to some of the shared understanding about The Boys' behaviours this also caused its own problems and these are discussed in the Appendix.

ONE

Young British Pakistani Muslim men and concern with increased levels of criminality

While young British Pakistani Muslim men are today frequently depicted as being violent, aggressive and closely associated with a range of criminal behaviour, they were once recognised as being on the whole law-abiding (Jones, 1993; Webster, 1997a; Marsh, 2006; Spalek, 2008). As Benson (1996) points out, despite the odd scare of illegal immigration, Britain's Asian population were seen as holistic, coherent and law-abiding, and were regarded as largely unproblematic. British Pakistanis were seen as more likely to be victims of crime rather than offenders (Maguire et al, 2007). In one of the earliest studies of ethnicity, *Asians and Crime: The Bradford Experience*, conducted by Mawby and Batta (1980), the British Asian community were commended for their low levels of offending behaviour and were perceived as being far less likely to be involved in serious offences than other groups. So the question that arises is why such a large number of young men from a religiously and culturally conservative Pakistani community are today turning to crime. There are even concerns today that factors which were previously regarded as protective against criminality for British Pakistani Muslims – such as strong family bonds, a sense of tradition, powerful religious faith – are now presented as causes, or at least facilitators, of criminality, and as being bothersome aspects of Pakistani culture (Wardak, 2000: Hudson, 2007; Croall, 2011). This chapter consequently examines the rise of this predicament; it starts by briefly examining Britain's Pakistani population before discussing some of the early incidents in which British Pakistani Muslim men came to be closely associated with criminality. It subsequently moves on to explore some of the potential reasons for the increase in the offending of young British Pakistani Muslim men.

Britain's Pakistani population

Large-scale immigration to Britain from Pakistan began in the 1950s, when Britain encouraged migration from the former colonies to satisfy its post-war labour needs. Initially men mostly in their twenties and thirties arrived to work in the UK but several years later Pakistani families also started arriving to the UK (see Chapter Two for a detailed history of Pakistani migration to the city of Bradford). Today the UK is home to the largest number of Pakistanis living in Europe. The British Pakistani population has grown from a mere 10,000 in 1951 to more than 1.1 million in the year 2011 (Census, 2011). A significant number of the British Pakistani population reside in England, living in cities such as London, Birmingham and Bradford. These cities today have thriving Pakistani neighbourhoods which include countless *halal* shops, traditional ladies' clothing shops and jewellery shops as well as large purpose-built mosques. The vast majority of Pakistanis are Muslims with small proportions who belong to the Christian faith. According to the 2011 census around 90% of Pakistanis living in England and Wales stated their religion was Islam (Census, 2011). The age profile of Pakistanis is today much younger than the average for England as more than half of the Pakistani population growth since 1991 is accounted for by those who were born in the UK (The Change Institute, Department for Communities and Local Government, March 2009). It is estimated that of those Pakistanis living in England, Wales and Scotland in 2001, 55% were born in the UK while 36.9% were born in Pakistan and 3.5% elsewhere in Asia (Dobbs et al, 2006). As mentioned, the British Pakistani population were in the past seen as coherent, law-abiding and largely unproblematic but starting from the early 1990s things were about to change and to do so considerably. This shift witnessed earlier concerns with African Caribbean to South Asian 'hyper-masculinity', with all the incumbent associations of threat, criminality and violence that this implied (Webster, 1996, 1997a; Goodey, 1998, 2001; Spalek, 2002a). Pakistani culture and the Islamic faith was increasingly demonised, coming to be seen as backward and in opposition to modern British values (Macey, 2002; Bolognani, 2009) and the next section of this chapter explores some of the early incidents in which British Pakistani Muslim men came to be closely associated with criminality.

History of the increased association of Pakistani men with offending behaviour

British Muslim men first came into the public eye for aggressive and violent behaviours in 1989 with the *Satanic Verses* controversy. The publication of Salman Rushdie's book had angered many British Muslims, witnessing Pakistani Muslims in Bradford burning copies of the book. Singh (2008) notes that it was only after the 1989 book-burning that British Muslim men started to be conceptualised as possessing a type of deviant masculinity, one that easily endorsed Islamic fundamentalism, along with other perceived negative traits such as aggression and the propensity for violence. Archer (2003) highlights that the *Satanic Verses* controversy also heralded a major shift in British debates around the politics of race and nation, provoking a debate over whether Britishness and Muslim identities were compatible.

In 1995, six years after the Rushdie affair, British Pakistani Muslim men again came into the public eye for aggressive behaviours, this time for their part in the riots that took place in Bradford (Alexander, 2000). The riots had started after rumours spread through the neighbourhood that a policeman had attacked a Pakistani woman, resulting in large groups of men (mostly young British Pakistanis) coming out onto the streets to demonstrate their anger and resentment at what they thought had been heavy-handedness by the police (Webster, 2007). However, an independent report into the Bradford riots commented on long-term problems in relations between the police and local British Pakistani youths, who were allegedly regularly subjected to 'inappropriate, unfair, or racist treatment by individual officers' (Allen and Barrett, 1996). According to Macey (2002) the police mishandled the situation by failing to understand the Muslim community and being unable to differentiate between genuinely concerned people and criminal gangs.

Criminalisation of young British Pakistani men was bought to the surface a few years later with the race riots in 2001. Although these riots took place in several northern towns and cities, the largest of these was in Bradford (Macey, 2002). Alexander (2004) highlights how, despite the Rushdie affair in 1989 and the 1995 riots, young British Pakistani men were still largely invisible in crime, but, following the 2001 race riots, there was a greater emphasis on their criminality. The cost of the 2001 Bradford riots was estimated to be £25 million (Bagguley and Hussain, 2003) and, as Macey (2002) contends, the riots left a dreadful impact on not only on Bradford but on the image of Pakistani Muslims in the UK. It was difficult to comprehend why young British Pakistanis who in the past were recognised for their law-abidingness could behave in this way, fighting with the police by rampaging on the streets, throwing petrol bombs, burning cars, smashing windows and looting (Hussain and Bagguley, 2009; Macey, 2002).

In the aftermath of the 2001 race riots, several commentators attempted to explain what the underlying reasons were for so many young British Pakistani Muslim men behaving in such aggressive ways. According to Denham's (2002: 1) Home Office report on the disorders, one explanation for the riots was identified as segregation, as Asian and White communities were living 'parallel lives'. Webster (2007: 105) similarly noted that 'the main basis of explanation and subsequent discussion about the 2001 disorders in northern English cities were claims of residential concentration, self-segregation and polarised (particularly Asian) communities'. David Smith (2009: 30) highlights that 'the supposed lack of integration of young Muslims in Britain, mostly of Pakistani origin, was already a concern of government even before the riots in the north of England in the spring of 2001'. High levels of unemployment and low levels of education were understood to be further explanations as to why so many young British-born Pakistani Muslim men behaved aggressively. Pearce and Bujra (2006) found that more than half of those convicted for their role in the riots had not gained a single GCSE, nor were they in either education or employment. However, many commentators would argue that during this time there was relatively little attempt made to understand what it was that was driving young British-born Pakistani men to be prepared to take on the police. There were perceptions of the riots which put the Pakistani community in a negative light, as if there was something innately criminal about being a young male Pakistani, rather than an analysis of the long, corrosive experiences of the community culminating in the riot. There was also a complete lack of understanding of the role of *Izzat* [respect, honour], of standing up for the safety and honour of the community by fighting for their patch, no matter how brutal the fight became. Questions were also raised in the aftermath of the riots regarding identity, Islamic faith, cultural practices, citizenship, belonging and integration and whether these were potential explanations for the offending behaviours. A number of smaller disturbances in which young British-born Pakistani Muslim men were involved followed the 2001 riots, but these were of no comparison with the race riots of 2001. From this point, British Pakistani Muslims were increasingly associated with the sale of drugs, particularly heroin and in the past decade or so for grooming white British girls as we discuss next.

Concern around drug dealing and cases of grooming white British girls

From 2001 onwards there has been an increase in the numbers of Muslim men, particularly those of Pakistani ethnicity, arrested for selling drugs, mainly heroin (see also Qasim, 2017). Home Office data relating to South Asian drug offenders in custody show a predominance of Pakistanis as opposed to Indians and Bangladeshis (Ruggiero and

Khan, 2006). While it is difficult to obtain precise figures for the numbers of British Pakistani men arrested for drug offences, there is nevertheless considerable media attention highlighting the surge in Pakistani heroin dealers. For example in 2017 35 criminals linked to a Bradford-based drug network were caught smuggling heroin into the UK from Pakistan in the lids of pens and were jailed for almost 200 years. In 2016 a West Yorkshire-based British Pakistani gang were jailed after shipping heroin from Pakistan concealed in boxes of tables. Drug conviction data revealed that, in Yorkshire and Humberside, more British Pakistanis were convicted for importing class A drugs into the UK over 2013 and 2014 than white British people and this, as Spalek (2002b) has previously suggested, may be related to the fact that, other than cannabis, heroin is the most common drug and Pakistani Muslims have ready access to it in Pakistan. Some commentators like Bolognani (2009) have even noted that, whereas in the past the drug markets in some Pakistani areas like parts of Bradford were controlled by individuals of African Caribbean origin, they have now been taken over by young men of Pakistani origin. The apparent increase in the numbers of young British Pakistani men trading drugs is not only worrying for the authorities but also, as a number of commentators have pointed out, it is deeply concerning for the Pakistani parent generation who see their youth turning to drug dealing as a way of making a livelihood (see Chapter Two for further discussion).

Another increased association with criminality relates to cases of Pakistani men grooming white British girls for sexual abuse. Gill and Harrison (2015: 34) state, 'Over the last four years, the United Kingdom (UK) has been beset by a moral panic concerning "South Asian men" grooming white girls for sexual exploitation.' There have been a number of high-profile cases in which British Pakistani Muslim men have been found guilty of grooming and have subsequently received lengthy custodial sentences. In May 2012, nine Pakistani men from the Rochdale area of Manchester were found guilty of sexually exploiting a number of underage girls. In February 2016, a Rotherham gang which groomed, raped and abused teenage girls was jailed for total of 102 years including 35-year term for the ringleader (BBC News, 2017). After cases of grooming in Rochdale in which Pakistani men went on to receive substantial custodial sentences, one report described the Rochdale cases as involving girls being 'recruited into sexual factory farming by Muslim men described as "pure evil" by detectives' (Pearson, 2012). These cases have clearly had a detrimental impact on the image of British Pakistani Muslim males and while it is difficult to prove whether or not Pakistani Muslim men are in reality involved in cases of grooming more than those of other ethnic groups, there is certainly, as Cockbain (2013) and a number of other commentators have highlighted, widespread media, public and policy debate around 'grooming', depicted as a new crime threat inextricably associated with 'Asian sex gangs' who deliberately seek out white British girls for repeated and horrific sexual abuse. As a result of the above-mentioned incidents, there is today increasing speculation that young British Pakistani Muslim men are much more criminal compared to those of the past. However, having said this, it is important to highlight again that it remains difficult to prove whether or not an objective increase in offending has occurred among the British Pakistani population and the extent to which the media has created this impression, as discussed next.

Have British Pakistani Muslim men really become more criminal?

There are clearly factors which have contributed to an impression of this group as likely offenders. As we discuss in this section, the process of labelling is considered a possible factor explaining concerns around the alleged increase in offending by young British Pakistani Muslim men. The labelling theory focuses on how and why society applies the label of 'criminal' to certain people, and the impact that this label then has on the behaviour of that particular person (Vold et al, 2002). According to Becker (1963: 4), 'Social groups create deviance by making the rules whose infraction constitutes deviance, and by applying those rules to particular people and labelling them as outsiders. From this point of view, the deviant is one to whom the label has been successfully applied; deviant behaviour is behaviour that people so label'. In other words, labelling theory maintains that powerful groups shape societal reaction by making the rules for powerless groups and enforcing them on people who have no power.

The media is considered to play a vital role in the process of labelling and stereotyping powerless groups – for example, by sensationalising stories about them and devoting such public attention to the issue that levels of anxiety within the mainstream public are increased. According to Cohen (1972), the media have long operated as agents of moral indignation in their own right. Even if they are not consciously engaged in crusading or muck-raking, their very reporting of certain 'facts' can be sufficient to generate indignation, concern, anxiety or even panic. This in turn creates moral panics which exaggerate the real threat posed by these groups, and which increases pressure on the government, police and courts to deal harshly with them.

It is mentioned that while African Caribbean people, through the use of image distortion and emotive language, were subjected to media distortions (Patel and Tyrer, 2011), there has been a growing shift from targeting black African Caribbean people to targeting those of Asian Muslim background (Kalra, 2003). Bhui (2009: 7-8) argues that, 'A brief perusal of the British Press (during 2007) reveals many prominent crime-related stories, mostly speculative and evidenced about Irish travellers, African Caribbean family structures, foreign nationals, and most vehemently, Muslims'. After 9/11 (attacks on the US in 2001) and 7/7 (London bombings, 2005), it is claimed that Muslims living in the UK have undergone a process that has seen them being regularly labelled as dangerous, terrorists, extremists and anti-Western (Patel and Tyrer, 2011). This process has, it is argued, resulted in the authorities targeting and hounding a significant proportion of British Muslim individuals (Patel and Tyrer, 2011) and subjecting them to processes of racialisation and criminalisation (Rowe, 2012). The notion of a suspect community developed by Hillyard (1993) argued that measures introduced by British governments in response to republican terrorism in Northern Ireland in the 1970s had resulted in all Irish people being conceptualised as potential offenders. Similarly, some commentators have argued that, in the same way, British Muslim individuals, due to measures introduced by the British government, are today considered to be potential criminals (Pantazis and Pemberton, 2009). Mythen et al (2009: 749) argue that it is expected that the UK should seek to reduce threats to public security through the range of powers at its disposal, but further argue that: 'the inequitable application of these modes of regulation have contributed to the wider process through which British Muslims are labelled as dangerous, risky "others" that threaten the security of the nation.'

Some commentators for this reason have claimed that the phenomenon of the British Pakistani Muslim individual as more criminal has a lot to do with events such as 9/11 and 7/7 (Patel and Tyrer, 2011), the argument being that, in the aftermath of these terrorist attacks, British Muslim communities have witnessed increasing levels of attention, which in return has raised suspicions of them (Archer, 2003). This attention is also reported to have intensified because of the murder of the British soldier Lee Rigby, figures that pointed to an increase in young UK Muslims travelling to Iraq and Syria to fight alongside the Islamic militant organisation ISIS (Cockburn, 2014) and, in more recent times, because of the 2017 London and Manchester stadium terror attacks. It is argued that because of intensified mistrust of British Muslim individuals, they are much more likely to be routinely stopped and searched by the police. Webster (2007: 109) states that, 'there is growing evidence that young Asian men are being disproportionately stopped and searched under the Terrorism Act'. In March 2005, Home Office minister Hazel Blears even declared that it was a fact of life that Asians and Muslims would be targeted more under anti-terrorism stop-and-search powers (Kundnani, 2006). It can therefore be argued that through stop and searches Muslim individuals are then discovered for crimes which previously went unnoticed.

It is also important to consider whether the reputation of the British Muslim individual as the 'enemy within' (Patel and Tyrer, 2011) has led the state to respond with harsher forms of policing and punitive measures when dealing with young British Pakistani Muslim men who offend and which is why it may come across that Muslims are more criminal. Critical criminologists argue that there is evidence suggesting that certain groups of people are treated differently in the forms of punishment given by the police and courts, which can add to the misleading image that they are more criminal than they are. There is evidence that black youths have, for a considerable time, been treated by the authorities far more harshly than white people. In a study conducted by Hoods, it was discovered that, regardless of whether they pleaded guilty or not, black defendants went on to receive longer sentences compared to white defendants (Webster, 1997b). Phillips and Brown's (1998) study, which was based on a sample of people arrested and brought to ten police stations in 1992-93, also found that ethnic minority suspects were more likely to be refused bail than white people with similar offences. Parallel to the black group, the British Pakistani Muslim group have experienced harsher punitive measures which, it is argued, adds to the image of them being more criminal. For example, the prosecution cases of the rioters in Bradford on 7 July 2001 saw immense discrepancies in the sentences given to Pakistani rioters compared with the more lenient sentences given to participants in other UK civil disturbances (Patel and Tyrer, 2011). Consequently, critical criminologists argue that crime rates provide a far from accurate picture of the actual extent of criminality in society, but increased police activity and suspicion can create a misleading image of a surge in crime among particular groups of people (Burke, 2009). Hall's (1978) study revealed that black individuals were portrayed as 'muggers' in order to take attention away from the economic recession the UK was then undergoing. This highlighted that the moral panic around black youth and their levels of criminality had a hidden agenda. So the question arises, in relation to the alleged increase in offending among second- and third-generation young British Pakistani Muslim men, whether there are other factors like this which need to be considered. According to Quraishi (2005: 119) there is significant historical evidence to assert that the construction of the Muslim as criminal or deviant is, in part, the cumulative outcome of policies, practices and prejudices (direct and indirect) that constitute Islamophobia.

Has there been an actual objective increase in offending of British Pakistani Muslims, or have changes in perception by law enforcement agencies resulted in a different approach to the community? Or do we find ourselves at some position along this spectrum? In order to establish whether young British Pakistani Muslim men are more prone to offending comparative studies of other communities will be required, but these remain to be done. Furthermore, trying to establish whether or not young British Pakistani Muslim men are more criminalised in comparison to other groups would require an examination of criminal statistics, but this is not a straightforward task as offenders from black and other ethnic minority groups are collectively categorised under the heading Black and Minority Ethnic (BME), which makes the task of highlighting or measuring crime committed by British Pakistani Muslim youth almost impossible to do. Croall (2011) on this issue argues that there is no simple way of categorising people into racial or ethnic groups as the widely used term BME has little specificity, and masks differences between Asian, African, Caribbean, Chinese and many other groups. Maguire et al (2007: 163), however, state that: 'Whether there is really an increase in Muslim Asian crime is, of course very difficult to know but there is certainly a rise in police stop-and-search, more imprisonment, suspicion, more division, and a criminalization which displays many of the features of the earlier criminalisation of African-Caribbeans.'

Socioeconomic and sociostructural factors explaining the increase in offending among British Pakistanis

This chapter has so far considered questions about the extent to which there is a significant increase in offending among British Pakistani Muslims and how far this perception might result from other factors. A number of theories have been put forward to explain the apparent increase and which we now discuss. Robert Merton's Anomie/Strain theory is considered an attractive explanation to explain the increase in offending among British Pakistani Muslim men. Merton (1968) concluded that poverty – or, in today's terminology, 'a negative socioeconomic climate' – has the potential to lead to a strain between the accepted goals of society and the socially approved means of reaching them – what he referred to as 'the strain theory'. Although this strain falls on a wide variety of people in society, it is more concentrated on those individuals who are from the lower class (Vold et al, 2002) and those individuals who are from ethnic minority backgrounds. It is well documented that, in common with black African-Caribbeans, Pakistanis are one of the poorest communities living in the UK. The extent of poverty among British Pakistanis is highlighted by figures which reveal that approximately 55% of Pakistanis living in the UK live in income poverty compared to black Africans (45%); black Caribbeans (30%), Indians (25%) and white British (20%) (Joseph Rowntree Foundation, 2007). Another reason why this strain falls heavily on the Pakistani group is because of their higher unemployment rates. Figures released by the Department of Work and Pensions and reported in the *Guardian* (Inman, 2014) showed that the jobless rate for young British Pakistanis was 45% and for young white people 19%. Some previous studies had even predicted that low employment levels among the British Pakistani group would see levels of offending increase in time (Mawby and Batta, 1980; Webster, 1997a). Macey (2002) in her study highlighted how a culture of poverty among the Pakistani population of Bradford was a possible explanation for why increasing numbers of Pakistani youth were turning to crime. Similar studies with Muslims in Europe have found that poverty is a key explanation for their offending behaviour. For example Sandberg and Pedersen (2011) in their study with Muslim offenders in Norway found that young men struggled to find employment and because of this sold drugs to make money. In the same way Bucerius's (2014) study with Turkish Muslim men in Germany found that the principal explanation for the men offending was because of the challenges they faced finding suitable employment. Similar studies in the US have found that where residents live in areas where few employment opportunities exist, there is greater potential for a segment of society to become socially isolated from the opportunities, resources and value system that are common outside these neighbourhoods and to turn to criminality.

A further sociological explanation is to do with parenting (Bolognani, 2009; Bari, 2014). Webster (1997a: 79) so rightly points out, 'It is the quality of parents' relationships to their sons and daughters which predicts the likelihood of delinquency, not the ethnicity of familial or parent culture'. A key documented finding of delinquency research is that delinquents are also less likely than non-delinquents to be closely tied to their parents (Hirschi, 2002). This is highlighted by evidence which has shown that those young people with weak relationships with parents and their family are much more likely to go on to offend (Farrington, 1978; Reiss, 1986; Sarnecki, 1986; Warr, 2002). It is reported that one reason for weak relationships has been communication breakdown, with the first generation of Pakistanis (the parental generation) speaking their native language and the second and third generations, those who were born and raised in the UK, preferring to speak English (Bolognani, 2009). Another aspect to parenting that could potentially lead young British-born Pakistani Muslim men into involvement in criminality is an absence of fathers. A large number of Pakistani fathers are known to work long hours which can mean that they are away from the home for considerable parts of the time, leaving mothers to bring up children on their own. It is documented that large numbers of Pakistani men are either self-employed running small businesses, particularly in markets, catering and taxi services (Dobbs et al, 2006). Bolognani, in her work on Bradford's Pakistani community, found that one of the most popular reasons given for offending by young British Pakistani men is bad parenting: Pakistani fathers, working unsociable hours, had unavoidably neglected their children who were growing up without guidance (Bolognani, 2009: 96). There is also concern that, whereas in the past Pakistani children, generally speaking, were known to live in two-parent households because the incidence of separation or divorce was much lower in this group (partly because of the stigma attached to separation; there is a steady change taking place as increasing numbers of Pakistani marriages are breaking down today (Ahmed, 2014)). Data from the 2001 census suggested a dramatic shift in marital instability and divorce among British Pakistani families, as the percentage of lone-parent families among British Pakistanis has doubled since the mid-1990s (Qureshi et al, 2014). According to the 2001 census, the number of lone parents among British Pakistanis was just below 20% (Babb et al, 2006: 24-25), whereas in 1994-95 lone parents accounted for just under 10% of all British Pakistani families (Allen and Barrett, 1996: 53). These statistics are indicators of significant marital instability among British Pakistani Muslims and could potentially mean that levels of offending among British Pakistani youth could increase even further in time given that it is well known that young people from single-parent families are more likely to be involved in crime because of the reduced parental supervision and activity with children among lone parents rather than the structure of the family as such (Graham and Bowling, 1995).

A further factor which potentially increases the risk of young British Pakistani Muslim men offending is living in households with large families, based on the argument that having a large family means parents have less time to supervise all their children, especially when they leave their household setting (Myers et al, 1987). Data obtained from the 2011 census suggests that the average Pakistani woman has 3.82 children while women born in the UK have 1.79 (Census, 2011). Given that considerable numbers of British Pakistani youth grow up in large households, parents can find supervising them a struggle and this may result in a greater risk of them turning to the streets and criminality.

Living in areas with high crime rates is a further sociostructural factor to potentially explain offending by young British Pakistani Muslim men (Marsh, 2006). Sutherland (1939) pointed to social factors which influenced delinquents to become involved in crime, positing Social Disorganisation theory, which became renowned for aiding many people's understanding of crime and delinquency (Glaser, 1960; Burgess and Akers, 1968; Curran and Renzetti, 1994; Akers, 1998). According to Sutherland (1939), crime was a normal process and had nothing to do with one's physical features, but was learned, just like other behaviours are learned. He argued that the key factor determining whether people violate the law is the meaning they give to the social conditions they experience rather than the conditions themselves. In other words, a person obeys or violates the law depending on how they define their situation (Vold et al, 2002). Most of the Pakistani population living in the UK, as mentioned, live in major cities – London, Birmingham, Leeds and Bradford – and largely in neighbourhoods which have high crime rates. The notion is that by living in these areas, British Pakistani youths are more likely to be exposed to offending behaviours than youths living in areas where fewer crimes take place, thus pointing to Miller's (1958) theory and the later theories of Shaw and McKay (1969) which have focused on delinquent youth being located in disorganised communities to explain the alleged increase in offending by young British Pakistani Muslim men. Previous studies with young Muslim offenders in Germany and Norway have highlighted how living in neighbourhoods with high crime rates is an important explanation of why young Muslim men become involved in crime (Sandberg and Pedersen, 2011: Bucerius, 2014). While an analysis of factors such as poverty, unemployment, poor education and overcrowding can potentially explain the increase in offending among young British Pakistani Muslim men, other explanations have focused on aspects such as the youthfulness of their demographic profile, as the age profile of British Pakistanis is much younger than the average for England (The Change Institute, Department for Communities and Local Government, March 2009). According to Webster (1997a), the sheer magnitude of the Pakistani youth population in the UK is quickly grasped when travelling around certain Pakistani neighbourhoods, as it is common to see large groups of young British Pakistani men congregating on the streets. The argument put forward is that, because young people is the most likely group to offend, a large British Pakistani youth profile means that increased numbers fall within the peak-offending age of 14-20 years (Webster, 1997a: 70). There were some commentators who, for this reason, had even predicted that levels of crime among British Pakistani Muslims were likely to increase in time (Quraishi, 2005).

Conclusion

This chapter has highlighted how young British-born Pakistani Muslim men are today increasingly associated with criminality. It has noted how a community which was once recognised as generally law-abiding and peaceful has come to be seen as being more criminal. This chapter has examined some of the early incidents which led to the Pakistani group moving from being perceived as law-abiding to being closely associated with offending behaviour. We have considered some factors which may have exaggerated the perception of criminality, such as the media and police attention as well as explored possible underlying reasons explaining the increased offending of British Pakistanis. However, despite a number of theories trying to explain the increased offending of this group, there is a significant gap in analysis which takes account of how young British Pakistani Muslim men see their actions or what their motivations are for offending. This is a dangerous situation for, without awareness or their own understanding, progress on resolving issues becomes a stalemate, leading nowhere. No initiative can work if the parties involved have not been heeded nor their perspectives understood or appreciated. Consequently, it is necessary to speak with young British Pakistani Muslim men who offend and attempt to understand their lives in order to establish the reasons why they offend. The present study subsequently aims to present insight into the lives of a social group of young British-born Pakistani Muslim men who are involved in a range of offending behaviours and who lived in the city of Bradford.

TWO

Bradford is home turf, it's our city

"We know people think Bradford's a shit hole because they think that there's too many Pakistanis living here and its always in the news for the wrong reasons but you know what, Bradford is a decent place to live, Bradford is home, it's our city, it's where we've all grown up, in fact it's the only place we really know" (Salman)

Bradford is situated in the north-west of England close to the Pennine Range and is a multicultural city where people of different backgrounds and ethnicities all live together. The largest ethnic minority community living in Bradford is the Pakistani group. It is estimated that one in five people (20.3% of the population) today is of Pakistani origin (Armstrong, 2012). Due to the city's substantial Pakistani population, it is at times referred to satirically as 'Bradistan' (Shackle, 2010). The Pakistani community has played a huge part in turning Bradford into one of the most important Muslim centres in the UK (Valentine, 2005). Today, one can find some of the largest mosques and influential Muslim leaders living in Bradford. The initial Pakistani migrants, however, arrived in Bradford to work in the thriving textile mills and this chapter starts by examining the history of this trade. The young men in this study reside in an area of Bradford called Manningham, and this chapter examines the historical circumstances which led to Manningham having the character it currently has. Also explored are the growing fears of crime committed by young British Pakistani men.

Textile Bradford

According to recent figures, Bradford has one of the UK's largest number of citizens, with a population of 528,200 (Office for National Statistics, 2015), although in 1801 it was a small market town with an estimated population of 6,393 (Office for National Statistics, 2015). The rapid success of the textile industry caused Bradford's substantial population growth as families from all over the UK and abroad arrived to work in the textile mills. Starting in the 1830s, migrants, predominantly from Germany and Ireland, arrived in Bradford.

Statistics reveal that in 1851 an estimated 10,000 of Bradford's residents were Irish (Hall, 2013). However, in the latter part of the 19th and the early part of the 20th centuries Bradford's thriving textile mills closed down due to increased competition overseas.

Unexpectedly, after the First World War Bradford again enjoyed textile success as those firms which had survived the difficult period of the late 1920s and early 1930s came to exploit a market which was growing again (Taylor and Gibson, 2010). Demand for textiles increased, and as Bradford already had a solid foundation in manufacturing, mill owners felt compelled to make the most of this opportunity. They were aware that they would need to operate aggressively and at maximum capacity if they were to have any hope of making money, especially since it was very clear that recovery in other countries would inevitably take place also. As a result, many mills in Bradford started operating around the clock, but in order to remain open for such long hours, mill owners had to find the necessary staff (Hall, 2013). Initially migrants from Poland, Ukraine and Yugoslavia arrived to work in the mills, but as soon as they could they would leave the unpleasant conditions in the mills for better jobs elsewhere. Consequently, mill owners were placed in a difficult situation, as they were on the one hand aware of the money-making potential of the situation, but at the same time realised the difficulty recruiting the workforce required to operate their mills. This led to mill owners recruiting from further afield – from countries such as India and Pakistan (formerly part of the British Empire) – and the history of this migration is well documented (Shaw, 1988; Lewis, 1994).

Pakistani migrants arrive to work in Bradford's textile mills

From the late 1950s, migrants from Pakistan arrived to work in Bradford. The migrants came predominantly from the Mirpur and Dadyal areas (Bolognani, 2009), apparently because nearly 300 towns and villages in these districts were submerged in the construction of the Mangla Dam, displacing many, and this led to the British and Pakistani governments making an agreement granting work permits to those who wished to come and work in the UK (Singh, 1994). Bradford witnessed a steady increase in migrants arriving from Pakistan to work in the textile mills. This increase is demonstrated by figures which reveal that in 1979 around 8% of the total workforce in Bradford was Asian and in 1981 this had increased to nearly 20% (Bolognani, 2009).

While mill work was considered unpleasant and low paid, and have antisocial working conditions, it nevertheless attracted Pakistani migrants. This was because in comparison with wages in Pakistan the wages, along with the long working hours in British mills, enabled the migrants to earn much more money than if they had been working in Pakistan. A large amount of their earnings was sent back to Pakistan to help support extended families (Riaz, 2004), so there was a need to keep living costs down. One way that the earliest Pakistani migrants did this was by living in shared houses. Some years later when the Pakistani migrants began inviting their wives and children to join them in the UK, they had to find larger alternative housing.[1] Many rented properties, but those who were in a position to do so purchased cheap inner-city properties which were situated close to the textile mills, paving the way for the creation of small communities where, for the first time, men women and children all lived together (Dahya, 1974). It is a natural form of social psychology for people of similar backgrounds to cluster together, as has been observed in many countries with migrant populations (Antonsich, 2014). In the case of the Pakistani population of Bradford, there were additional factors which accelerated and strengthened this process. Among these factors were language difficulties, dietary and religious requirements and, quite frankly, a sense of protection and security in the face of a hostile and racist dominant majority, as we discuss later in this chapter.

Textile demise made life difficult for Pakistani migrants

The late 1970s and early 1980s saw the demise of Bradford's booming textile industry as textile mills slowly went out of business (Hall, 2013), attributed to a rise of cheap textiles from the Far East. The demise of the textile trade led to mass unemployment and an economic decline for Bradford (Singh, 2002). The Pakistani migrants who had relied so heavily on the textile industry were now placed in a very difficult financial situation, pondering what they should do next. Should they return to their homeland Pakistan or stay here?

It was not as simple as packing their bags and returning, as the vast majority of Pakistani migrants had made some important decisions. Most had invited their wives and children to come and join them and had by now purchased their own properties. Furthermore, their children were attending local schools and more importantly, they appreciated the free health care which was provided in the UK, all of which meant that moving back to Pakistan was no longer an easy option for them. Din (2006: 31) explains, 'the idea that immigrant men would "return home" was quickly dismissed after the early men experienced the advantages that Vilayat (UK) could offer them and their families'.

Given that the vast majority of Pakistani migrants who had arrived to work in the UK were uneducated, having had very little schooling in Pakistan, they consequently struggled to find alternative employment (Riaz, 2004). A considerable number of these migrants became unemployed. Some who could drive turned to the taxi trade and those who were more business-oriented and were financially independent decided to go into business. Bolognani notes (2009: 62) how Pakistani-owned businesses grew exponentially 'from a mere five in 1959 (of which were: two food stores with a butchers attached, and three cafes) to 133 businesses in 1966 (which were: 51 food stores and 16 cafes) to 260 by 1970 increasing to 600 by the year 1978, 35% of which were in Manningham'. A considerable number of the initial Pakistani migrants who came to work in the textile trade lived in the Manningham area of Bradford. This is also the area in which The Boys in the study reside, and the next section provides a detailed picture of this neighbourhood.

Manningham

Manningham, situated only a few miles west of the city centre, is known for its rich heritage of housing and exceptional design. One of the prominent sites of Manningham is the renowned chimney of Lister Mills which towers high above the countless rows of small, neatly planned terraced houses that surround it. In its heyday the mill was one of the largest silk factories in the world (Oake, 2012). However, due to the demise of the textile trade, large parts of the building are in a derelict and abandoned state today. Lister Park, situated alongside Keighley Road, is another popular attraction in Manningham. Both Lister Park and Lister Mills were built by Samuel Cunliffe Lister (1815-1906) who was a successful and wealthy textile manufacturer.

The textile industry has clearly left its mark on Manningham, from the build-up of the neighbourhood to its residents. Considerable numbers of the original Pakistani migrants who arrived in Bradford chose to live in Manningham because of work. Manningham Mills, Valley Mills, Lumb Lane and Whetley Mills were all located here. Another reason for settling in Manningham was because properties here were considerably cheaper than those in other parts of Bradford. This was attractive for the Pakistani migrants as it is reported that banks were reluctant to give mortgages to people of Pakistani origin (Bolognani,

2009), which correlates with the fact that the Islamic faith discourages Muslims from dealing with moneylenders on an interest basis.

Another factor which encouraged the early Pakistani migrants to live in Manningham was the fear of racism. In the 1970s and 1980s Bradford's Pakistani community experienced an increased number of racial attacks, which were blamed on the economic decline and escalating unemployment for Bradford's residents. The British National Party (BNP), in its attempt to try and stop immigration, launched a propaganda campaign and 'Paki-bashing' was common during this period. This refers to occasions when groups of white men went around neighbourhoods smashing the windows of houses and cars that they thought belonged to Pakistani residents. Consequently, such incidents left the Pakistani community cautious, fearful and vulnerable (Alam and Husband, 2006), and for this reason many Pakistani families decided to live near one another as doing so made them feel safer, secure in the knowledge that their fellow Pakistanis would look out for them. The sense of fear, poverty and discrimination all led to a powerful sense of solidarity, of mutual concern, among the community, reminiscent of and deriving from the sense of village life, where survival itself depended on people supporting and protecting each other (Riaz, 2004). There was also a curious sense of continuity in that the first generation of Pakistani migrants had been used to such a strong and close-knit village community in their homeland, a sense which was perpetuated and recreated in an alien land for different reasons. This strong and close-knit sense of community and solidarity was passed onto the second and third generation, with people still looking out for each other.

Today the older generation, the primary Pakistani migrants (also known as the elders) who moved to Manningham from Pakistan to work in the textile mills, have mostly retired, and for these individuals the close-knit community of which they are a part offers them a relatively busy and active social life. A typical day consists of traditional activities such as meeting friends and relatives to converse, especially about developments in Pakistan, visiting friends and family in their homes, attending the mosque and performing traditional *Puree* [paying respects to those who have lost a relative]. Today Manningham, with its vast Pakistani population and its wide range of shops (*halal* butchers, Asian ladies' clothes shops and Asian jewellers) caters for the needs of the large Pakistani community. Nonetheless, it has its fair share of problems, and we discuss some of these next.

Manningham – far from a haven of peace

Key among the issues that affect Manningham are deprivation and poverty, considered to affect large numbers of its residents. Despite many of Manningham's Pakistani residents having bought their own properties, they are nonetheless some of the poorest in the neighbourhood. According to Anil Singh, director of the Manningham Housing Association, 'it used to be thought that owner-occupation was an indicator of wealth and prosperity but the reality is quite different'. High levels of owner-occupation among the ethnic minority population have been achieved at the huge social cost of massive overcrowding and extremely poor conditions. They simply do not have the resources to maintain or repair their homes (*Telegraph and Argus*, 1999).

Manningham also has a huge problem with unemployment, with significant numbers of its working-age citizens unable to find work. Despite once having been a magnet for employment, the picture today is very different as Bradford today has one of the highest unemployment rates in the UK. In 2010 the figure was 5.2% for Bradford compared with 4.2% nationally (Joseph Rowntree Foundation, 2011).

It is reported that unemployment affects Bradford's Pakistani residents more than those who are white or from other ethnicities, as Alam and Husband (2006) noted. While unemployment has affected many in the city, the Pakistani group have struggled with unemployment ever since the closure of the textile mills which they were heavily dependent on. There are few opportunities left in Bradford and, in common with The Boys, many others in the city feel frustrated that Bradford is failing to attract large businesses. Throughout the study The Boys would frequently talk of how Bradford had very little when compared to neighbouring Leeds. One afternoon as we were sat in the car, Tanny, clearly annoyed with the bleak situation in Bradford, started telling The Boys that he was contemplating moving away:

> "There's no money left here. All the big companies have left, and Bradford has just got smaller and smaller and Leeds has got bigger and bigger. Look at Westfield shopping centre – it's been left abandoned for years, no one gives a shit. You just got people here who don't care, but who like to make out they do."

In one sense Tanny can be seen as a peripheral character among The Boys, yet at the same time the sentiment he expressed here was widely held by them. Interestingly, it was noted that people of all generations throughout the neighbourhood expressed the same or similar views. It could be argued that it was felt with more intensity by The Boys because they felt more constrained to remain within Bradford for family reasons in comparison with other people of equivalent age in other communities.

Problems with overcrowding in Manningham

A further issue facing the area of Manningham is overcrowding. According to the 2011 census the population of Manningham was 19,983 (Census, 2011). A considerable number of the large properties that were once lived in by mill owners and managers have been converted into multiple bedsits and flats, while in other cases they give the impression of abandonment, being run down and some in near ruin. The small terraced properties, many of which are back to back and were built for mill workers, have also perpetuated conditions of overcrowding, thus creating tension on a number of fronts, car parking being of key concern for many of the area's residents. One characteristic of Bradford, which is also apparent in areas other than Manningham, is that the properties were all built in the 19th century when transportation was either by foot or horse-drawn omnibus. Over the last 50 years car ownership has become widespread, to the degree that it is normal for some homes to have multiple car drivers and owners in residence. Each car owner wants to park in front of their own home, but the streets were not designed to allow this, and most homes do not have frontages which are suitable for converting to parking spaces. With parking spaces at a premium, considerable tension can erupt, especially if a family is seen as being selfish in trying to bully their neighbours by parking vehicles in front of their neighbour's houses.

A recent influx of Eastern Europeans into the area has added to the overcrowding problem and has created further tension. Although at one level this appears to rectify the imbalance, it has in reality intensified divisions, as the Eastern Europeans are now objects of hatred not only to sympathisers of racist groups but also to some young Pakistanis who perceive them as a grave threat to their housing and employment prospects in an already depleting and depreciating market. In a report conducted by the Joseph Rowntree Foundation (Hudson et al, 2011), titled *Recession and Cohesion in Bradford*, it was reported that tensions have arisen with the arrival of the new European Union (EU) communities between them and the established Asian community in Bradford. Stories occasionally circulate the neighbourhood about fights between groups of British Pakistani youth and Eastern European families.

Generational tension between Pakistani elders and youth

Generation tension between Pakistani elders and the youth is apparent in the neighbourhood. There is a sense among Manningham's older Pakistani residents that the younger generations have begun to rebel strongly against traditional ways. This tension is in part because of a clash in cultures as Webster (1997a: 81) explains: 'Tensions exist between the generations with the first generation eager to maintain the values and customs practised back in the country of origin; and the younger generation (mostly born in this country) unaware of and indifferent to the original culture'. It appears that considerable numbers of Pakistani parents have tried to maintain strong cultural groundings by trying to raise their children in the same manner in which they were raised but this in itself has created conflict as their children struggle to reconcile their British identity with an identity that their parents are trying to uphold. Some commentators have highlighted how British Pakistani youth for this reason often live double lives, whereby they adhere to cultural/religious norms in the home and community, but lead Western lifestyles away from the home (Anwar and Hussain, 2014).

This generational tension means that the Pakistani community of Bradford no longer has the influence it once did over the actions of so many of its youth (Valentine, 2005). This tension has been previously suggested as a possible explanation behind the riots that took place in Bradford in 1995 and 2001 (Din, 2006). Another possible reason for this tension may be the age gap between the elders and youth. Other suggested factors are because the elders, who grew up in Pakistan, have had different experiences compared to their youth, which means that they are often oblivious to the challenges that their youth experience (Bolognani, 2009). This is partly because, unlike the parental generation, their children have grown up in the UK, have attended school, learned to speak English as their first language and in many ways prefer Western culture to that of their parents. Meanwhile, a further matter which affects the neighbourhood of Manningham, as well as affecting a number of other parts of Bradford, is segregated communities and social isolation.

Living in segregated communities

When discussing the diverse communities that shape Bradford, a concern that is often heard is that Bradford is one of the most segregated cities in the UK, as confirmed by Professor Ted Cantle, who wrote a report on the causes of the 2001 riots (BBC News, 2011). This concern is frequently highlighted. In an article in the *Guardian*, Samia Rahman stated that 'one aspect of racial segregation in Bradford that provoked huge concern across all communities was that of segregated secondary schools. Examples of a school being all-Asian while the school down the road was mostly white were depressingly common' (Rahman, 2009).

Some argue that a process of self-segregation has taken place, whereby Pakistanis – for social, cultural and religious reasons – have settled together. Bradford's Pakistani residents, however, argue that the segregation of their communities is not down to them but instead attributed to 'White Flight' (Phillips, 2002; Dorling and Rees, 2003; Valentine, 2005), a term used to refer to when white people leave particular neighbourhoods. The Boys were well aware of the extent of segregation in their neighbourhood, and would often talk of the reasons why so few white British people lived in their area. In the third year of the study, while I was hanging around on the street corners with some of The Boys, Yass spotted a 'For Sale' sign outside the home of the last remaining white British person living on the street. This started a discussion, with Yass asking the others why it was the case that white British people had all moved away from their area. Ilyas replied:

> "They don't like living near us, they think we give their area a bad name. Listen to this, 'bout ten years ago, me uncle bought a house and there were white people living on both sides of him but then guess what happened, after 'bout six months the lady next door put her house on the market and some *apnas* [Pakistani] bought it and then a bit later, the other side put their house on the market and some more *apnas* bought it."

Although Ilyas's perception was simplistic and distorted, nevertheless the fact is that there was a sense that, as the *apnas* took over a neighbourhood, it was easy for them to do so because of white dislike of Pakistanis. There was a narrowness of focus here that fuelled mutual suspicion, hostility and misunderstanding between the whites and the

Pakistanis, which expressed itself with the self-justifying response which Ilyas's comment epitomised.

Meanwhile, of all the Pakistani neighbourhoods in Bradford, Manningham is often considered to be one of the most segregated. It is an area where very few white people live today. According to the 2011 census, over 75% of its residents are Muslims (Census, 2011). Incidents such as the riots in 1995 and 2001 have, according to many, led to increasing segregation between the Pakistani and white community. Some have even gone as far as to say that Manningham is today a no-go area for whites. This was highlighted in an incident in which the local newspaper described how a young Pakistani man attacked a white male while shouting "Manningham belongs to Muslims. We don't want whites. We rule Bradford. We are going to get you out." He subsequently received a five-year prison term (Wright, 2009). Although incidents like these are few and far between, they nevertheless leave a lasting impact on Manningham, creating further segregation between people of different ethnic and religious backgrounds. This sense of awareness of the speed of transition in the community and the deep anxiety it raises has not just been noted by The Boys themselves. Many of the Pakistani elders have voiced concern and noted how the area has changed from when they first arrived. Although there was occasional racism, in the past Manningham, according to them, was considered a more stable and generally peaceful community. Now there is a rising sense of menace and a growing sense of fear of crime among many of its residents.

Fear of crime

One of the key signifiers of change in Manningham and in Bradford generally is the rising fear of crime. There are concerns that crime is increasing, and on a scale that has not previously been seen. Bolognani (2009) refers to a new wave of crime committed by young British Pakistani men and highlights how this is worrying not only for the authorities, but also many of the Pakistani elders. In *Crime and Muslim Britain*, Bolognani (2009) highlights that Pakistani Britons are consumed by fear, not so much of racism and its effects, but of the drug dealing, gun crime, gangs and domestic violence they believe that young British Pakistani men are liable to get involved in. In the same way, in Spalek's *Islam, Crime and Criminal Justice* (2002b), Macey (2002) highlights in her chapter how increasing numbers of young British Pakistani men in Bradford are involved in criminal activities and that their acts of aggression have become part of everyday life. Spalek and

Lambert (2007) cite the view of the Muslim Council of Britain that there is a risk that a generation of young British Muslim men will be criminalised. There are concerns, too, about violence on one another as Pakistani-on-Pakistani crime seems to have increased. This has seen turf wars take place between rival groups of young British Pakistani men from the neighbourhood, some of which are linked to drug patches with dealers fighting dealers and at times using guns. There is speculation of an increase in the number of gun-related crimes, not only in Manningham but in Bradford as a whole, with young British Pakistani individuals both perpetrators and victims. The Think Tank Reform ranked urban areas with populations of more than 100,000 using data on burglary, murder, rape, robbery, car and gun crime from the police, and Bradford came top of the list for gun-related crimes (BBC News, 2006). The Pakistani community share such concerns – the elder generation frequently voice their fears about increasing crime in their neighbourhood. This was highlighted in a research project conducted on Bradford's Muslim community in which Valentine (2005) revealed that 54.9% of residents interviewed ranked crime as the main problem in the area, while 52.4% of them believed they were likely to be victims of crime during the coming year.

Concern with drug dealing in Bradford

Bradford is one of a number of places in the UK that have acquired a reputation as a city with a severe drugs problem (Alam and Husband, 2006). Whether the scale of the problem is, in reality, more severe in Bradford than it is in other cities is questionable. However, Bradford, and in particular certain areas of Bradford are recognised as having a close affiliation with drugs and drug dealers. For example, some neighbourhoods are said to have drug dealers standing around on the streets and selling drugs in a somewhat ordinary fashion. This was highlighted in a recent case in which Judge Roger Thomas QC spoke out when sentencing Class A drug dealers who were caught under Operation Stalebank by stating that, 'Street dealing in heroin and crack cocaine was so commonplace in parts of Bradford, it was almost considered the "social norm"' (Loweth, 2013).

The area of Manningham had a reputation as a being a place where substantial drug activity took place, so much so that The Boys themselves would jokingly say, "If they [drugs] ain't in Manningham then they're probably ain't anywhere." Jameel: "It's impossible for anyone to live around here and not know anything about drugs. It's like you see 'em everywhere."

The authorities have the same perception, and Manningham is considered a hotspot for illegal drug activity. In sentencing a drug dealer, Judge Alistair McCallum spoke out about Manningham, claiming that: "One million pounds of heroin is sold on Manningham Lane every day... It is a shocking situation and a lot of our young folk are ending up as heroin addicts" (Carter, 2002). A considerable number of young British Pakistani Muslim men living in Bradford are today involved with drugs. The exact number is of course difficult to verify but there is certainly, it seems, increasing numbers being sentenced for drug-related crimes over the past decade. This has seen concern, as Bolognani (2009) and other commenters have noted that it has now become popularly understood that, whereas in the past the drug market in Bradford was controlled by individuals from Afro-Caribbean origin, it has now been taken over by men of Pakistani origin. Significant numbers of young British Pakistani men in Bradford are understood to sell on the streets at the bottom end of the drug-dealing spectrum and one reason for this is that demand for drug dealing is so high that one can easily move in and out the drug-dealing circle, unless and until caught.

Concern with drugs in the neighbourhood in which The Boys lived was so prevalent that the Pakistani parent generation were repeatedly reminding their youth of the damage that drugs could do to them. Martin Wainwright, who looked at the deep roots of cultural conflict lying at the heart of the Bradford's Asian community, similarly found that the Pakistani (Asian) parental generation were constantly voicing concern about drugs, strongly feeling that drugs were a danger to their community (Wainwright, 1995). Meanwhile Bolognani (2009) states that one of the findings was that the main problem affecting Bradford's Pakistani community was considered to be drugs. Even within the local mosque, the Imam [religious leader and teacher] would try to deter British Pakistani youth from becoming involved with drugs. This was made apparent when one afternoon I attended the local mosque to pray *Jumma* [Friday prayers] along with some of The Boys. On entering the mosque, The Boys took off their shoes, placed them on the racks and casually walked into the large prayer room, making their way to the very back of the mosque. Sitting on the mosque floor was clearly uncomfortable for The Boys so some, like Ali, found resting their backs against the wall and stretching their legs to be more relaxing. A few local youths who The Boys knew came over to sit next to them, whispering in conversation, careful not to disturb worshippers who were praying nearby. It quickly became apparent that *Jumma* was not only a time for The Boys to attend mosque for worship, but also an opportunity to catch up with friends who they had not seen all week.

Ali and Jameel start laughing, amused by what Ahmed was whispering to them, when Salman noticed that a number of the elders sat ahead of them were looking at them in disgust. "Boys, quieten it down, they [elders] staring at us, *kasmay* [honestly]," he whispered to the others. The elders, as The Boys were aware, considered it to be extremely disrespectful for anyone to be talking so loudly in the mosque.

A short while later, the Imam stood up, and The Boys sat up suitably so as to focus and listen to what he had to say. In his sermon, the Imam started off by talking about Islamic values, which, as he explained, were crucial for Muslims to abide by, before moving on to talk extensively about the local area. He passionately made his view clear that one of the biggest problems facing the community today was drugs, saying how in his view drugs were a problem not only for British Pakistani boys, but that some of the area's British Pakistani girls were also involved:

> "I see brothers and even young sisters using drugs, selling drugs like they are doing nothing wrong. They forget that they are *haraam* [forbidden], and I swear to you that the money that they are making from them [selling drugs] will benefit them nothing on the day when they will stand in front of their lord. Trust me, on that day they will plead and ask Allah to forgive them but no, it will be too late then."

The Imam then advised the youth who were in the mosque to attend a talk which would be held in a nearby mosque entitled 'Do you want to be a bad boy?' This talk, as the Imam explained, would be delivered by a young charismatic speaker able to relate with the youth, and who would try and deter them from a life of crime.

It was clear that the local mosque held strong feelings about drugs, considering consumption or any involvement with them to be *haraam* [prohibited within their Islamic faith]. The Pakistani elders in the neighbourhood were also aware of the dangers that drug consumption carried, mindful that certain drugs had the potential to take control over the body. In addition, they were also aware that any involvement in drugs had the potential of affecting the family *Izzat* [honour], giving the entire family a bad reputation in the eyes of the community.

Another example of the Pakistani elders' view on drugs was when one day I was standing by Zaks [shop] along with some of The Kids. Yass asked if anyone had seen a particular individual from the neighbourhood who only a few days earlier had been released from prison when they noticed 'Uncle' walking towards them. "Hide it, Uncle's coming, hide it," Yass whispered to the others, who stamped out their rolled-up joints and swiftly placed them in their cigarette boxes. Initially I thought that this individual may have been a literal uncle of one of The Kids, and it took me some time to realise that he was not related to any of them, but instead a man of senior years whom they respected. Within the community it was commonplace to refer to respected male elders as 'Uncle' and to ladies as 'Aunty'. Uncle stopped, he shook hands with us, and then asked how we were doing before moving on to ask what some of them were doing with their lives. The Kids were aware that to tell Uncle that they were unemployed would encourage further dialogue. Yass: "I'm working at the checkout at Morrison's, Uncle." Zahir tells Uncle that he is working as a manager of a shop in town, at which stage Uncle replies: "You think I'm some old man who's stupid. I know what you do, my son, you don't need to lie to me. I used to be young like you one time, let me tell you."

Uncle then started giving some advice. To anyone else it would have seemed like friendly guidance, but The Kids found it to be annoying as they really did not want to listen to what he had to say, particularly when they were getting 'stoned', as they were smoking cannabis:

> *Uncle*: "Your youth only lasts for a short while, don't abuse it. You want to try and make something of your lives, you want to work hard and achieve something with your lives. You know, when I was your age, I worked in two jobs. I worked 14 hours a day, every day."

Uncle then told the boys that they should refrain from using drugs: "Keep away from drugs and alcohol. They are for people who have no hope in life."

Fortunately for The Kids, the conversation with Uncle had to come to a halt as the call to prayer could be heard, and he was on his way to the local mosque. This conversation, however, highlighted difficult tensions within the community based on intergenerational divergence. The life experiences of the first generation of Pakistani migrants who settled in the UK were of hard graft in the mills, but the concept of Bradford as 'Worstedopolis' died before the young men in the study were born. Although the culture of respect for elders still survived among some, it was disappearing among their younger successors. Often when the elders are reminiscing with the hope of inspiring the youth to live honest lives by hard work, some second- and third-generation British Pakistanis are deaf to their recollections, as was the case above, remaining unmotivated by the modesty of their vision of life, that of honest work and poor pay. Instead, they prefer to take shortcuts and, in the case of some, this involves turning to drugs as a way in which to make quick money even when they are fully aware that in the eyes of their parents and wider community, drugs are considered as being *haraam*.

Conclusion

What emerges from an examination of Bradford is a combination of factors. First, notwithstanding the fact that today Bradford is a city with a large population, some areas like Manningham have the close-knit feel of a village, and yet at the same time a village with an international perspective. Many areas of the city (Manningham being typical in this regard) have been settled by Pakistanis who derive from the same ancestral area, who know each other and are family-related. Manningham is closely bonded together by ties of culture, tradition, ethnic identity and religion.

Outwardly, the Pakistani community appears to be thriving, yet there are huge underlying problems which are often ignored. There is tension between the newly arrived Eastern European migrants who have moved into Manningham, alongside existing tensions between the Pakistani elders and second- and third-generation Pakistani youth who have lived dissimilar lives. Whereas the primary Pakistani migrants who arrived to Bradford found work relatively easily in the textile mills, many of the younger generations, those born and raised in the UK, have struggled and this in itself has created frustration on their part. Bradford is seen as offering the youth very little in terms of employment opportunities, but while The Boys are perfectly capable of saying that 'Brady' [Bradford] is 'shit', at the same time they say that they could not live anywhere else.

The portrayal of Bradford in the media (much like other cities) has definitely compounded many of its problems, the most significant of which are high unemployment, intense poverty and overcrowding. For example, Steve Emerson on Fox News recently described Birmingham as a no-go area for non-Muslims. In doing so he misrepresented the truth and reality of the situation in Birmingham (BBC News, 2015). This exposed the scale of media negativity towards cities with dense populations of Muslims, which, of course, includes Bradford ('Bradistan'). Although this may seem amusing to outsiders, it has had a damaging effect on the city – for example, in deterring potential employers. It leads to the 'spark and tinder' theory that where existing underlying problems reach a sufficient level of severity, it only takes a trivial event to create a serious disturbance. There is a risk of this being the case in Bradford, and of The Boys or their successors being caught up in any confrontations. There is a risk of serious disturbance being created through The Boys' own endeavours to protect their patch, to establish status for themselves, and to give vent to years of pent-up frustration and anger at the injustices they have endured. Home turf is an area of decayed grandeur, disappointed hopes and ever deepening despair.

Note

[1] Due to the *Commonwealth Immigration Act 1962* on primary migrants, Pakistani migrants invited family members, including their wives and children, to live with them in the UK.

THREE

The Boys, their identities and dynamics

This chapter investigates the identity, substructures and dynamics of the young men known as The Boys. The chapter is divided into sections which describe each of The Boys and which discuss aspects of their behaviours and personalities in more depth. The Boys were a social group of young British-born Pakistani Muslim men aged 25-33. Among The Boys there was what one could refer to as a core group (made up of nine individuals) and a more fluid, marginal group (made up of five individuals) whose social lives overlapped with The Boys, but who at other times conducted their social lives independently and at some distance from them. In addition, there was a third group which consisted of five younger males aged 18-20 who were variously referred to by The Boys as The Kids or 'the younger ones'. This group of young men were in many ways replicating the lives of The Boys and we discuss who they were and their relationship with The Boys further on in this chapter.

The Boys were a well-known group of friends, recognised locally by other young people, elders and even the local shopkeepers. This was to become apparent early on in the study when I accompanied some of The Boys on a walk through the neighbourhood to their

The Boys and The Kids

Core Boys

Bash Nav
Salman Shaf Ahmed
Ali
Jameel Kamran Afzal

Marginal Boys

Umar Bilal Tanny
Mehmood
Imaran

The Kids

Yass Majid
Ilyas Wahid
Zahir

local phone shop. On the way they stopped several times to speak with people who they knew, greeting a group of elders stood near the mosque with the Muslim greeting *Aslaam Alaikum* [peace be with you] later acknowledging youths on the other side of the road by simply nodding their heads before stopping to talk with several young men whom they knew.

One reason why The Boys had this level of familiarity in the neighbourhood was because, as discussed in Chapter Two, the local Pakistani population formed a close-knit community. This would see some of the Pakistani elders occasionally referring to one of The Boys by their father's name – Son of Wahid or Son of Khan, for example. Some of The Boys' families were also incredibly close in their friendships, as was the case with Nav and Salman, who would walk into each other's houses as though they were their own. When one day I asked whether they were related, Nav replied: "Nah [no], we're not cousins or owt [anything], it's just that my family and Salman's family have known each other for ages. When we were small, he [Salman] used to always come to our house with his mum and that, and ever since then we've been like family."

One of the strongest characteristics of the neighbourhood's Pakistani community was that, for a variety of reasons, there was a strong sense of mutual support, both psychologically and practically. While this was clearly an obvious response for first generation migrants in an alien and largely hostile land, this characteristic seems to have continued on down through the generations.

Membership to the social circle of The Boys

The Boys could be split into two smaller groups, with one group considered the core and the other the marginal group. The most significant difference was that those referred to as the core group would hang out together more often than the Marginal Boys. In addition, the Marginal Boys were, it seemed, far less likely to be involved in delinquent behaviours, whereas the core group continued to offend. This is well illustrated by Burke (2008) who suggests that a small group of offenders continue to offend well into their adult life while others desist. Nevertheless, between The Boys themselves, any distinctions made no practical difference to the way they saw each other: if you were one of The Boys then you were one of The Boys, no matter how often or how rarely you hung out.

Membership of their social group appeared to be quite straightforward. In order to be considered as one of them, you had to have known each other for some time, have hung around together and have demonstrated solidarity to each other. As loyalty and solidarity were significant aspects of their friendship, and there is considerable previous research which similarly suggests that solidarity is the delinquent group's primary character (Giordano et al, 1986; Chu et al, 2012).

It was normal for The Boys to share stories depicting their unified support while hanging out together. These stories were often told to remind others that they had stuck by them and that they expected the same if and when such an occasion arose. At other times they were told to show appreciation or even to have something to talk about. One evening as we were sitting in Jameel's car, The Boys having 'a smoke' [smoking cannabis], Shaf, who was drinking alcohol, started telling the others of how he "had a lot of love" for Jameel. He then reminisced about a time when he had been attacked by a group of boys from a nearby neighbourhood and how Jameel had helped him: "If it wasn't for Jameel, I would have been knocked the fuck out. He came out of nowhere and just laced into one of them, he gave him a right blow across the face, knocking him to the floor."

Solidarity among The Boys

There was a particular and outstanding solidarity between The Boys which transcended blood kinship and all other barriers. Where such a close bond existed, The Boys would refer to each other as *bhai* [brother]. They would even talk of each other's parents as if they were their own, reinforcing their alliance to one another. The Boys replicated solidarity often in ways similar to the parental generation who formed their own tight-knit communities, as discussed in Chapter Two. Previous studies with young offenders have noted how their shared identity can often provide them with an advantage in terms of establishing trust and solidarity (Grund and Densley, 2012). In the same way, shared identity, shared ethnicity and religious identification created a powerful sense of solidarity among The Boys.

Ahmed and Salman were two of The Boys who were incredibly close friends. They had been friends since primary school and would over the course of the study demonstrate considerable solidarity with one another. Salman, unlike most of the other Boys, spent a lot of time working out in the gym and was forever trying to convince the others to go with him, but this usually fell on deaf ears. Although the other Boys would occasionally work out, they appeared less keen on wanting to spend their time in this way. But Salman loved the gym, and was especially conscious of his food intake, in particular the need to consume food which was high in protein. Having said that, there were times when he would abandon his usually strict diet in order to show solidarity with The Boys by sharing food with them, but this then made him the butt of their mockery – for example, Ali telling Salman "I thought you were on a diet blud [bro], you're back on them chips, you twat [idiot]."

Ali was someone who The Boys referred to as a 'joker', as he was almost constantly playing pranks on the others, with his target a lot of the time being Shaf. Personality-wise, however, Ali was a very complex individual because even though he would fool around from time to time, there were many times when he would be surprisingly reflective. Psychologically this is not an unusual personality construct. Often profoundly sensitive and reflective men will conceal their sensibility behind a humorous exterior – the so-called 'tears of the clown', whereby the joker of the pack is also the most sensitive. Ali's most outstanding quality was his sense of decency, honour and solidarity to The Boys, which was not apparent to those who did not know him well but permeated his every thought. He had a strong code by which he lived and with which he treated others, even when joking around with them. This would often be demonstrated when hanging out with The Boys. What can be seen here is that among The Boys there was great diversity of character and personality; but notwithstanding that, there was a strong sense of cohesion that overrode personality differences. Meanwhile, another feature that stood out in the lives of The Boys was their attitude to and relationships with women, and we discuss this in more detail next.

Don't take relationships with women seriously

The Boys' understanding of relationships with women was that one should avoid getting into a 'proper' relationship but instead have 'a bit on the side'. There were a number of reasons why they chose not to take their relationships seriously. There was, for some, a realisation that being in a relationship had the potential to change behaviours. In addition, The Boys generally viewed the girls who they knew or with whom they hung out as 'slappers' and 'slags'. Many a time they would speak negatively of these girls and express how they felt that most of these women had been 'with half of the men in Bradford'. There was an astonishing obliviousness to the double standards at work here, since The Boys would take up with girls and enjoy their company, yet be sexist towards them. The idea of it taking 'two to tango', with both being on an equal moral footing, was not a perception that The Boys understood. There was considerable peer pressure between them to behave flippantly with the women with whom they associated and see them as sexual objects rather than as equals. However, despite the attitude that most of The Boys demonstrated towards women, Ahmed was in some ways different from the other boys. He had feelings for his girlfriend, although this was never something that he would openly admit to any of the others. But there were occasions when he would make excuses that he had other things to do, or would even disappear without telling any of The Boys where he was going. One evening, as we were walking through the park, Ahmed received a phone call. He answered it, and stopped walking with us. The rest of us continued walking, as we were under the assumption that Ahmed would catch up with us on finishing his call. To The Boys' disbelief, they realised that he was nowhere to be seen. They knew why Ahmed had left sheepishly: he had gone to meet his girlfriend. Salman furiously said to Kamran: "He's gone to see that fat bitch again, he's never gonna get his head out of her arse. Man's fucking blind." As we continued walking Salman mentioned how, in his view, Ahmed would never learn, and he even questioned whether his girlfriend was being faithful to him: "He's never changing; he's always been like it, he just gets shafted [used] by them and they just take him for a right ride. Bet you anything she's fucking someone behind his back."

The Boys clearly did not like Ahmed, or any of the others, leaving them to go see a girl. In their eyes it was wrong to openly admit that any of them preferred to spend time with their girlfriends rather than hang out with The Boys.

Ahmed was a particularly interesting character. Unusually for The Boys, he was exceptionally romantic and caring, and formed deep attachments to women. At the same time, he made disastrous choices in the women to whom he gave his love and loyalty. Thus on the one hand he experienced disapprobation from The Boys, who thought he should 'fuck 'em and leave 'em'; that women were commodities to be used unemotionally, just for the physical pleasure that could be derived. On the other hand, he repeatedly chose unsuitable women, so time after time had his heart broken when he discovered that they were, in fact, using him for his generosity and supportiveness while going behind his back to have liaisons with other men. Ahmed stood out in particular for his supportiveness towards the children these women had already had from previous relationships. He had the gift of treating them as if they were his own. It was painful to see him caught in this way and becoming more hurt as time went by and he repeated the same errors of judgement. He slowly came to believe that it was women in general who were at fault and not to be trusted, rather than acknowledging that it was his own choice of specific women that needed to be adjusted. A further feature among The Boys that characterised their behaviours and lives was issues with anger, as we now discuss.

Anger problems were prevalent among The Boys

Previous research with young male offenders has shown how they have higher levels of anger compared to non-offenders (Sukhodolsky and Ruchkin, 2004) and this tendency was certainly evident among The Boys. A low level of emotional intelligence was a characteristic of a significant proportion of The Boys, and they were quick to resort to violence as their way of resolving issues. They were unable to see that such violence almost always exacerbated the original problem. Although Shaf was a relatively quiet person who generally only spoke when spoken to, he would, in the words of The Boys, "get brave when drunk". Shaf had a temper problem. He would often deliberately stare at people in an aggressive and threatening manner, and there were countless times during the study when he would get drunk and start behaving aggressively, shouting and swearing uncontrollably. It was common for some of the other boys to even at times deliberately wind him up, considering it amusing to then see Shaf 'go off on one' [get angry].

In the same way to Shaf, it did not take much to see Kamran lose his temper, and in doing so he often turned to violence. There were even times when some of the other boys were incredibly wary of him, cautious not to say anything that could upset him. Kamran was a blunt type of character: he was known to be direct, and to say exactly whatever was on his mind. In one instance early on in the study he found himself in a heated argument with someone from the neighbourhood. The argument had escalated after Kamran had told the other person, rather openly, that he thought that he was a 'prick' [idiot] and that he didn't like him. Several weeks before the study, after an argument with his girlfriend, Kamran smashed her house up. On another occasion he was involved in an incident with a few of the local lads. The incident had started when a group of boys had parked their car outside his house and this had annoyed him to such an extent that he decided to follow them in his car, resulting in a confrontation. Later that evening, while hanging out with some of the others at Bash's flat, Kamran received a phone call from his father telling him that his car windows had been smashed. This infuriated him even more, as he was convinced that it was the same boys with whom he had been involved in a fight earlier: "They don't know who I am, I'm gonna deal with 'em, fuck that, no one gets away with smashing my windows. I know it's them fucking little shits, they ain't got the bottle to come see me, they know I'll fuck them up."

Kamran now wanted revenge, and there was a risk that this feud could go on until someone was badly hurt. Jameel was another of The Boys who appeared to have anger problems. He had a solidly built physique and an intimidating appearance, but most of the time he was a pleasant individual. Having said that, he did like to portray himself as a 'bad boy', even down to the way in which he drove his car. A few months before the start of the fieldwork Jameel was in a fight with someone due a road-rage incident. On another occasion, this time during the study, as we were standing by his car one afternoon, Jameel saw someone drive past, and he hastily jumped in his car and appeared to follow him. We watched on and after a short while he drove back to where we were still standing, got out of the car and in an aggressive way told us that he was going to get him one day: "I'm gonna fuck that bastard up; he ain't got any tatte [bottle] to come fight me, has he? Is he gonna hide for the rest of his life from me?"

I later found out that the reason why Jameel wanted to hurt this particular individual was because, after having fought with him previously, this particular individual had smashed Jameel's house windows. Jameel was not the type of person to let things go, and was annoyed that this individual did not have the courage to fight him and was running scared. In his attempt to try and calm Jameel down, Ali said: "Bro, forget him, he's regretting it man, I bet you he is. Did you see his face? He looked fucking scared or what. If I was you I'd just let it go now, bro, get him to pay for the windows and fuck it."

Ali's response here showed the extent to which The Boys would go to if they were angered by the actions of others. There was pressure on them to perpetuate feuds and to win at all costs. This was especially true where reputation and material goods were at stake.

Meanwhile, Bash was another of The Boys who appeared to have temper issues. He would lose his temper often, but this generally appeared to be with those whom he was able to intimidate. He had a tendency to pick his fights, so to speak, aware that to pick a fight with someone stronger than him may mean risk of defeat. In short, Bash's life experiences had turned him into a bully. Bash was also referred to by some of The Boys as 'old school'; he was a few years older than the other Boys and was considered to be someone who had 'been there and done it'. According to Bash, there was nothing that he had not done, which was clear from listening to his many (and often over-exaggerated) stories. Although Bash was a number of years older than the other Boys, one would never have assumed so, as he looked younger than most of them and had also had a tendency to behave childishly. Bash, like so many of The Boys, enjoyed considerable banter, which sometimes could be childlike.

Banter was common among The Boys

The Boys would frequently enjoy banter; in fact it was almost expected whenever they got together. They would try to outdo one another in their mockery, and comments were at times offensive, but this was typical behaviour among a group of young men who knew each other exceptionally well. It is well documented that banter among men is extremely common: as Lampert and Ervin-Tripp (2006: 52) point out, 'Men are said to be more likely to tell jokes, especially jokes with sexual and aggressive themes.' The fact the banter was often aggressive and offensive was linked to the sense of machismo The Boys had. The idea that anyone would show sensitivity would be interpreted as a failure of masculinity and make the individual a target for being picked on. Therefore there was an invisible boundary: banter could not be too aggressive, as it would spill over into confrontation; nor could it be too gentle, as it would spill over into a failure of masculinity. All of The Boys would banter in the hope of outscoring each other with offensive comments, and in doing so try to make the others who were listening laugh. Afzal was one who would be on the receiving end of considerable banter from The Boys. There were even times when banter would lead to The Boys doing silly pranks. There was one particular occasion during the study when Ahmed, Jameel and Salman were bantering with Afzal, telling him somewhat aggressively how lazy he was. They then decided to teach Afzal a lesson, and physically picked him up and forced him into the boot of Ahmed's car. They then drove around with him in the boot until Afzal pleaded to be let free. The Boys found it hilarious, particularly when Ahmed drove the car at speed around sharp corners and suddenly slammed on the brakes so that Afzal felt the force of the car braking. Afzal was one of few boys who appeared to have mental health concerns as we discuss next.

Underlying mental health concerns

A number of The Boys demonstrated personality traits which seemed to link with underlying mental health issues, which may explain some of their behaviours. Previous research suggests that young offenders are three times more likely to have a mental health problem when compared with the general population (Harrington and Bailey, 2005). Research also suggests that ethnic minority offenders have higher rates of post-traumatic stress (Harrington and Bailey, 2005).

Afzal was not someone you would have naturally placed with The Boys. He spent most of the day sleeping and was considered by The Boys to be a 'lazy shit'. Afzal also suffered from mood fluctuations: there were occasions when he appeared outgoing and upbeat, but other occasions when he could be down and depressed. This would suggest a psychiatric condition but he had not explored this, nor had the others suggested it being worthy of investigation. It is fair to say that acknowledgement of mental health in the British Pakistani community is stigmatised. Previous research has found that there is fear, shame and secrecy surrounding mental health issues among the Pakistani community in the UK (Rethink, 2006). As a result of such stigma those with mental health problems would often be endured rather than encouraged to seek appropriate medical help. The Boys would sometimes talk about people they knew and had grown up with who were in 'The Mount' [Lynfield Mount, a mental health hospital in Bradford]. It seemed that for this reason, The Boys did all they could to ensure that Afzal was encouraged to spend time with them. They felt that spending time on his own had a negative impact on him and his mental state. As a result, The Boys were not prepared to take no for an answer from Afzal. There were times when they would resort to going into his house and physically dragging him out of his bed. The Boys were friendly with his parents, and Afzal's father himself would sometimes encourage them to wake Afzal up and get him to go out.

Nav was someone you could call an adrenaline junkie. He was always involved in what The Boys referred to as 'crazy shit'. Having been banned from driving, he continued to drive and was careless about getting caught by the police. He had been arrested for dangerous driving on countless occasions, and had been in prison so often that he could not remember the exact number of times. In some ways it appeared that Nav was more childlike than the others. Frequently he would be seen driving his car through the streets like a maniac, going as close as possible to other cars, and even showing his road rage to some of the younger boys congregating on the street corners. There was a side to Nav which in some ways set him apart from the other boys. He was a lot more emotional than them, and The Boys thought he had not been the same since his father's death several years earlier. There were times when hanging out that he would become emotional, particularly when talking about his father.

The Boys on the fringe

A number of The Boys appeared to be loosening their connections with offending and in some ways also with The Boys. These individuals, for the benefit of the study, are referred to as marginal members and this section explores the explanations for them not spending as much time as they once did with The Boys. It also explores the identities and personalities of the Marginal Boys more closely.

The marginal group consisted of five individuals who had grown up with The Boys and who had, over the years, spent considerable time hanging out with them but gradually drifted away and ceased associating on a regular basis. It was apparent that, for some of the Marginal Boys, their lives went in a slightly different direction to the core group. The turning point for some of The Boys came at school-leaving age, as was the case for Bilal. He was someone who stopped hanging out with The Boys as often as he used to when he reached the age of 16. His father became fearful that he could end up in prison and consequently enticed him to work for the family business. Bilal remembers getting arrested in town for shoplifting when he had told his parents he was at college. On the way back home after attending the police interview Bilal recalls his dad telling him, "There's no more college for you. You're working every day from now on with me. You can say goodbye to education." Since then Bilal had worked in the family business and now helped his father manage it. Even though he spent most of his time at the business, Bilal would still find time to hang out with The Boys.

Others from the marginal group got married in arranged marriages and soon after started their own families. Umar was someone who, according to the others, was 'under the thumb'. The Boys would often mock him by claiming that he was only allowed to hang out with them when his wife was away at her parents' house. Umar had got married when he was 18 and spent most of his time with his family. Mehmood and Tanny were also married. Both of these Boys had been involved in delinquency, but had eventually moved away from hanging out with The Boys all the time, resulting in desistence from offending. At the age of 18, Mehmood's parents had arranged him to marry a girl from Pakistan. Today he was in a stable relationship, living with his wife and children, so for this reason he limited the time that he spent with The Boys. This supports the argument as made by Sampson and Laub (1995) that marriage or being in a relationship can allow the offender to step back from his peer group, having the potential to stop him from further offending.

In some cases, a sense of the onset of age and maturity can explain the Marginal Boys' desire to lessen involvement in certain activities that could cause trouble. For others it could be the acquisition of responsibilities such as jobs and families which, as Blumstein and Cohen (1987) argue, promote desistence. A further explanation may have been reflection on the problems being experienced by friends who persisted in such activities. All encounters with the courts left a long-lasting shadow over the lives of The Boys, but for some there was the realisation that the fewer problems with the courts the better their chance of achieving a normal and straight life.

Given that the Marginal Boys were well respected and trusted, this enabled them to move in and out of the circle as they pleased. The general view among The Boys was that once you were one of them you remained so unless, of course, you did something that went against their principles.

While the Marginal Boys had desisted from offending behaviours, it is worth mentioning that there were times when some of them would behave just as delinquently as the core group. This highlights Farrington's (1997) argument that there is always a risk that those who have desisted will go on to reoffend. There was instead today a new group of young men who were coming through on the streets, young men who were in their late teens and who were referred to by The Boys as The Kids or as 'the younger lads' as we discuss now.

The Kids – a younger group of Boys coming on the streets

The Kids lived in the same neighbourhood as The Boys. Some of them were related to The Boys: Wahid was Afzal's nephew, and a few of the others were distantly related to Salman and Tanny. While the social group of The Kids was extensive, those who The Boys were friendlier with were Zahir, Majid, Wahid, Yass and Ilyas. These boys were unemployed and spent considerable amounts of their time socialising on the streets. It is important to point out that although The Boys had a level of friendship with The Kids this was, in some ways, rather restricted, as The Boys did not like to be seen by others in the neighbourhood hanging around with any of The Kids, or even standing on the street corners with them. The reason for this was because the streets were viewed by The Boys as the place for The Kids and no longer a place for them. As The Boys perceived it, standing on the street corners at their age (in their mid- to late twenties) was embarrassing; as they felt that it would give others the impression that they were 'down and out' [had no money and nothing better to do].

The Boys, however, were in many ways role models for The Kids. The Kids aspired to be just like The Boys, and for this reason they would imitate many of the things that The Boys did. The Kids showed great admiration for The Boys as they felt that many of them had 'street cred', and for this reason they tried to replicate their behaviour. While walking around the neighbourhood one afternoon with Ali, we bumped into Yass. Yass was one of the younger boys who hung around the streets frequently – in fact, whenever we drove past in the car we were sure to see Yass standing near Zaks [shop], sometimes with others and even at times on his own. On one particular occasion Ali stopped his car by the shops and asked Yass "How's Wahid doing?" (Wahid had only recently been sentenced and was in prison). Yass replied:

> "I spoke to him the other day, he says he's doing all right and that, he's up north [referring to the prison he was in]. He's a dopey shit though, used to think he's clever but he weren't clever. People who are clever don't get caught. Look at me, I've never been down [in prison] and I been doing KoKa [selling cocaine] for a while now."

Yass was clearly trying to impress Ali, as was often the case with The Kids. Too often they would try and impress The Boys by showing them that they were not scared and were on the ball when it came to making money. The Kids aspired to be like The Boys and wanted to please them and earn their respect and The Boys, it appeared, loved the admiration that they received from The Kids. However, this also had a curious effect on The Boys as it made them very conscious of their age and the sense that they were being edged off the street and were no longer the dominant group. There was one particular occasion later on in the study when an argument broke out between one of The Boys and one of The Kids. This started from some messing around in which Nav took Wahid's phone and then refused to give it back to him. Wahid was annoyed that Nav would not give him his phone back, and was conscious that he [Nav] could go through his messages. "Give it to me you dickhead, give it back, its mine not yours", shouted Wahid at Nav. This quickly turned into a heated dispute from which both were clearly not prepared to back down from. "Who the fuck you talking to like that, I'll slap you, you twat, [idiot]" said Nav, at which point Wahid started losing it – "Go on hit me, go on, I'm not scared of you" – while continuing to swear at Nav. "I'm not hitting you as there's too many faces around, I will come find you," Nav replied calmly. Later that evening Nav turned up at Wahid's house, adamant that he wanted to teach him a lesson, for, as he put it, "getting funny with me". However, as both families knew each other, they helped sort the issue out without anyone getting hurt. Although it was rare to see any of The Kids challenge The Boys, there was a sense that some of them felt that they were no longer prepared to tolerate any disrespectful behaviour from anyone.

Do a job for us?

While the relationship The Boys had with The Kids was in many ways restricted, this did not stop them from trying to get some of The Kids to do occasional crime-related jobs for them. Previous research has highlighted how it is a common theme for adult offenders to lure adolescents into involvement in crime and particularly into drug dealing (Taylor, 1990). The types of crime-related jobs that The Boys would entice The Kids to do could range from smashing someone's car windows to dropping drugs off to waiting customers. In return The Boys would look out for or even protect The Kids, ensuring no one troubled them and, if anyone did, coming to their defence.

It was to become apparent how The Boys would look out for The Kids when, one day as I was with The Boys driving through the local area, Zahir (one of The Kids), who was standing by Zaks, flagged us to stop the car. We stopped, and Zahir explained that a person known to them had punched him in the face. Salman was furious at what he heard, he could not believe how this particular person would hit someone so much younger than him and responded angrily to Zahir: "Don't worry bro, I will deal with him, he's a fucking mug. I will show the short-arse cunt how to hit kids."

Salman saw this person a few days after the discussion and interrogated him about the incident. He soon learned that the reason why Zahir had been beaten up was because he had sworn at this person's mother. On hearing this, Salman decided to leave the discussion at that, but warned him that if he ever was to lay his finger on Zahir again then he would not be so kind to him. One of the qualities of The Boys that was difficult for outsiders to understand was that, although they were involved in criminal activity, there was a deep sense of morality and honour which pervaded their street culture. A key element of this was the respect shown to elders, and particularly to women within the family, especially their mothers. This was both a religious and a cultural attitude. The Prophet Muhammad taught that 'paradise lies at the feet of your mother', and deriving from that teaching is the idea that mothers should be treated with extreme respect. Therefore, the idea that anyone would disrespect anyone's mother was considered an extreme offence within the community. In summary it can be seen that the relationship between The Boys and The Kids was reciprocal to varying degrees, but usually to the advantage of The Boys, whom The Kids wanted to emulate, but The Boys viewed The Kids as being more criminalised than them, they were seen as being more ruthless in many ways and prepared to take risks. Another factor that encouraged The Kids to impress The Boys was that it was only through imitating such behaviour that they felt they could achieve prosperity as well as status. Since there were so few legitimate avenues to wealth, status and material goods, the very few opportunities take a lot of time, in contrast to the instantaneous results of crime, encouraging The Kids to mimic the actions of the older ones. One particular reason why the young men felt that there were few legitimate avenues to wealth was because they had very poor educational backgrounds, and the next section explores the reasons for this.

We have very little education

While the young men in the study obtained few if any qualifications, Pakistani youth in the UK on the whole have, it seems, made the least progress when it comes to educational achievement. Webster (2007: 124) states: 'Although for most ethnic minority groups the second and third generation have made significant educational progress – especially some ethnic groups such as African, Asians, Sikhs and Indians and African-Caribbean women – Caribbean, Pakistani and Bangladeshi boys have made least progress.'

There are a number of factors which have contributed to why British Pakistani youth have struggled with achieving educational standards, as we briefly discuss here. Poverty is understood as being one explanation (Modood, 1997). As discussed previously, Pakistanis are one of the poorest groups living in the UK. This was also apparent among The Boys, who came from deprived households and lived in a deprived neighbourhood. Parents having low education levels are further explanations why second- and third-generation British Pakistanis have struggled with achieving educational achievement (Burnhill et al, 1990) and this was apparent among The Boys whose parents had little, if any, qualifications. Parents unable to speak English fluently, creating barriers to communicating with schools and supporting their children in school is another explanation (Gillborn, 2002; Sharp et al, 2004). According to some commentators, a further reason why considerable numbers of British Pakistani youth have not done as well as other groups in terms of educational achievement is because of there being more of a focus on business than education amongst this group. In her study, Bolognani (2009) found that Pakistani groups in Bradford happened to have a more of a business-oriented mentality than an education-oriented one. This in some ways was also apparent from observation of the lives of The Boys. The Boys took a keen interest in business, they would on occasion discuss of setting up business themselves but this never transpired.

Some of The Boys did not even get as far as taking their GCSEs. Nav was excluded at the age of 14 for fighting. Afzal was also excluded for fighting, Jameel just didn't bother turning up for his GCSEs and Ahmed, who was only entered for one GCSE, did not turn up either. Ali went to Pakistan at the age of 15 because his parents felt that his behaviour was becoming uncontrollable. As for the others who did complete school, these boys achieved low grades. Shaf admitted that, when he discovered that his GCSE results were not good, before he went home he took a detour via the local library where he altered his results, and then went home to show his parents the forged rather than the real results.

Those of The Boys who did go onto study at sixth form and college later dropped out, either because they did not like the course or they were excluded. Ahmed, who had only been given a place in the school's sixth form because his father had pleaded with the deputy head to give his son a chance, lasted only a few weeks. He was later excluded for stealing another student's mobile phone, but he could not understand why the school excluded him when the incident had taken place off school premises:

> "Me dad had to beg the deputy head to let me come back and I was really happy he gave me a chance but then they kicked me out. It wasn't even like I did anything in school, we were near Toller Lane and I saw this guy who was in school with me, he was a right cheeky fucker in school so I taxed [stole] his phone and told him to do one, and I then I got kicked out [of school]."

Due to his poor behaviour at school, Salman went on to study at college as the school did not allow him back into the sixth form. However, he only lasted a month in college before he was excluded for fighting with another student. Shaf, who went on to do a business course at Bradford College, told me that he spent more of his time in the arcade shops than at the college and later dropped out.

In addition to the lack of education that The Boys obtained while they were at school, I learned that school was the place for initiation into their offending behaviours, as is highlighted by self-report surveys which show that a sizable minority of young people are involved in offending behaviour when they are still at school (Graham and Bowling, 1995; MORI, 2004). The next section of this chapter examines the offending behaviour among The Boys while they were still at school and discusses how truanting from school led The Boys to become involved in criminal behaviour.

Schooldays and delinquency

Although The Boys were now in their mid-twenties, they remembered their schooldays well; The Boys would frequently discuss them while hanging out, fondly reminiscing about their experiences of school. Schooldays were generally seen by The Boys to have been 'a good laugh', a time when they built friendships, misbehaved and regularly played truant. Previous research has noted how truancy is a stepping-stone to delinquent and criminal activity in young males (Farrington, 2002; Hayden et al, 2006). While school was considered to have been a pleasant time by The Boys, some remembered it as a place where there was tension and hostility between groups of British Pakistani boys and groups of white boys.

> *Ali*: "Every day we used to fight against the *goras* [white lads]. It was proper nuts at school, they were mainly from Haworth Road sides, proper racist fuckers and some days they used to get the better of us, and other days we would get the better of them; there used to be bare [a lot of] tension."

Experiences of racism led to a need to stick together and demonstrate their loyalties to fellow Pakistanis when dealing with hostility from racist pupils. The racist tension they experienced at school and the perceived need to resort to violence in a school environment were clearly features of early adolescence for The Boys. Salman, who attended a different school – one closer to the area in which The Boys lived and which was predominantly attended by Pakistani students – remembered school as an enjoyable time:

> "Schooldays were a buzz, *kasam se* [honestly] I used to get up, get dressed, jump onto bus then I'd meet the boys near

top park. We'd make the plan for the day, then we'll all go to class and sign in so the teacher sees us in, then just like sneak out for the day, go to town and that."

Salman continued explaining how while truanting in town The Boys would get involved in delinquent behaviours: "We'd go to Boots and spray nice aftershaves; then we'd go around just shoplifting and chilling, we'd just chill mostly in Kirkgate [shopping centre]."

Delinquency was admired when The Boys were in secondary school, and, as previous research has noted, it is when a child is at secondary school that there is a greater risk of becoming delinquent as this is when most juvenile convictions occur (Graham, 1988; Farrington, 2002). Parker's (1974) ethnographic study *A View from the Boys* highlighted how young men would offend while they were still at school. Truanting from school and spending the day in town led some of The Boys to get involved in fights, as was the case for Ahmed who recalled his first ever fight being in Bradford town when truanting from school.

"I was knocking off this one time and this *gora* [white person] bumped into me, so without thinking or anything, I just turned around and punched him twice in the face. Next minute he was out cold, he was laying on the floor, you know what, I was shocked to see him drop so quick, I felt like I was Mike Tyson or something." [Laughs]

While truanting, some of The Boys would routinely get up to 'daring acts' and this could even be as extreme as stealing cars and driving them around school in order to try and impress their peers. One evening as we sat in Bash's flat, some of them were recalling how they would drive the cars that they had stolen into the school car park. Kamran: "We were mad ones playing hide and seek (with the cars) around the school, should have seen man's faces at school."

The Boys recalled a time when they were arrested in stolen cars near to the school.

Ahmed: "*Mawe* [police] were watching us from this house, they then waited for us to be in the cars and then all a sudden they jumped on us."

Salman: "Should have seen it, there was about nine of us in the cells, we were shouting like fuck in there [police cells], doing the cops heads in."

On another evening while hanging out at Shah's girlfriend's flat, The Boys started talking about their days at school, the conversation having started when Shah was proudly telling his girlfriend how he had 'knocked out' [beat] a particular individual at school who was now living nearby. He asked the others whether they could remember seeing the fight. The conversation quickly moved on to a number of other fights that some of The Boys were involved in, and Ahmed then asked them if they could remember when he stole a teacher's handbag before explaining how he had stolen it:

> "It was break time and I sneaked into her class, I looked around and there was no one there so I went to her drawer and saw her bag and quickly looked through it, grabbed her purse and chipped [ran] before someone saw me, the next thing everyone was getting blamed in the class." [Laughs]

The Boys quickly became disillusioned with school itself and stopped making an effort and yet many of them demonstrated very high levels of intelligence. They applied their intelligence to surviving on the streets and to entrepreneurial skills, sometimes within and often outside the law. The majority of The Boys were presently unemployed and there were several reasons why this was the case. One explanation was, of course, their lack of educational achievement, another, however, was their selectiveness about which jobs they felt were suitable for them, as we discuss next.

Work can't affect 'street cred'

This section examines why The Boys were incredibly particular about the type of jobs they were prepared to undertake, one reason being that The Boys had a different outlook on work compared with their parents who, as we know, were prepared to take any job that generally came their way, often working long, strenuous hours in underprivileged conditions. The Boys felt that mill work, takeaways or restaurants were good enough for their parents and their cousins, but such jobs were not suitable for them. Quite literally, in The Boys' eyes nothing was worse than degrading, dead-end work. In the search for street credibility, most of The Boys became very selective about the types of jobs they were prepared to do. Some of The Boys hoped to find decent, well-paid jobs, jobs that carried credibility such as, for example, working as managers of shops. Elliot's study as early as 1962 noted how it was common for delinquents to associate managerial or professional jobs with success in life, but did not anticipate obtaining them. Subsequent studies have similarly found that status is fundamental among young males who offend and which motivates them to pursue a criminal career instead of finding employment (Emler and Reicher, 1995). Bash and Shaf made it quite clear that they would rather remain unemployed than work in jobs which were poorly paid, referring to low-paid jobs as being more suitable for *mangies* [a nickname for people who have newly arrived from Pakistan] or for Eastern Europeans than for them. Bash was proud of the fact that he had not worked and he would often make it known that the type of job he was prepared to undertake had to be one which was well-paid and one that did not affect his standing on the street.

One evening when as I was at Bash's flat and the other boys went out to buy some 'smoke' [cannabis], I noticed how different Bash was on his own – far less boisterous, and a lot more open about himself with me. His cooker was not working, and I got the feeling that he was struggling to make ends meet financially, although I was aware that he would not admit this openly in front of the others. It was a point of pride for many of The Boys to appear to be financially stable. The idea that the others knew that one was impoverished was perceived by many of them as shameful. They would rather be in denial about their frail financial situation than to admit poverty with a risk of losing face. When I suggested to Bash that perhaps he should find a job, while he seemed interested, he reminded me of his requirements:

> "I'll never work in a job that pays basic wage. Don't get me wrong, if I find a job that pays like three or four hundred pounds a week, I'll take it but you know what, I won't even get out of bed for anything less than it, you must be mad to think I would."

I was intrigued to know why, and Bash explained that: "If you do then you make yourself look like a right crank [fool]. What's the point in trying to make a name for yourself then just throwing it away."

Clearly, image and reputation were tremendously important to The Boys, as a number of them mentioned that they would not work in a job which interfered with their standing on the street. Similarly Rivera and Short's study (1967: 89) reported that in Chicago boys will refuse or quit jobs which interfere with gang life, and 'the long hours on the corner with customary pursuits of wine, women and "rep" are involved in tardiness and absenteeism which contribute to job failure'. Street cred was immensely important, and for those of The Boys who considered themselves to have it, it was crucial to maintain it. The Boys felt that by working in low-paid jobs they could seriously jeopardise their standing on the street. This became apparent to me one day when Ali and Shaf, who were parked in their car waiting for some of the other Boys, were talking about how someone they knew had recently been released from prison. This person, who was considered to have built a good name for himself – that is, had credibility on the street – was now working in a warehouse:

Ali: "I seen Raza, he was coming out of Farmers Boy [warehouse]. I didn't know man would get a job in there?"

Shaf: "I think he's gone all straight and that, I spoke to him and he was like, fuck this shit, I just want to keep me head down. He's getting too old for going in and out of prison, eh?"

Ali: "Yeah but it's *baseti* [insulting] to work in there, he was meant to have a name for himself."

The Boys felt that one way of enhancing their reputation on the streets was when they were able to make money illegally or without working very hard for it. They would frequently speak about who from the area was 'smashing it' [making a considerable amount of money illegally]. Those individuals who were making money illegally would even boast to others, saying how much they had made, as was the case with Kamran, who, in the first year of the fieldwork, proudly told me how he was making good money from selling drugs: "I'm making money right now as I speak to you; I got man's driving around for me who I pay a wage to. They bring me the paper [money] at the end of the night."

Kamran had what The Boys referred to as 'a round', a name given to a delivery business of selling drugs. How it works is that one gives their phone number to people who they think are on drugs, and when they receive a call the drugs are delivered to them. This was clearly a complex and well-organised business, but it was not a legitimate one. There were even conversations among The Boys about how some youth in the neighbourhood would build their line [get as many phone customers as possible] and later sell the phone line on to other drug dealers.

Conclusion

What becomes clear from this chapter is that The Boys are a diverse group of friends who through their shared experiences and identity have formed strong attachments. One of their strongest characteristics is the solidarity they demonstrate to one another. This solidarity is born from a need for survival, to the ability to uphold self-worth in what they perceive to be a hostile environment. Meanwhile what also characterised The Boys was happiness in life, a boisterousness that was often without any harmful intent but which could be seen as daunting to people who did not know them personally. The vigour of their speech, the earthiness of vision and expression, the loudness and the larger-than-life quality was common to all of them. At the same time, their experience of hostility from others (especially outside the community) made them quick-witted in their response and determined not to show any weakness whatsoever to anyone. In turn this led to a level of aggression which bubbled under the surface and broke out very quickly. It led to confrontations within the group, as mentioned, but also allowed The Boys to bond together, especially when faced with any perceived threat from outside. The Boys showed considerable business skills, although they were applied to criminal activities. They showed intense loyalty to each other. They showed a strong moral sense with regard to family values. In so many ways they showed qualities that are deemed desirable in society. However, having once been given a criminal record, this stain proved indelible. Once the label of criminal had been attached, that label became a master status so the sentence in some ways forced them back to the environment they were in beforehand, thus effectively guaranteeing reoffending, for which The Boys would find themselves blamed.

FOUR

'We are hustlers' – relationship with drugs

As discussed in the previous chapter, The Boys sold illegal drugs and this chapter examines how they would go about their drug dealing [hustling]. Selling drugs was a risky business, so in order to evade detection from the police The Boys had to go about trading them discreetly. Drug dealing also involved shrewdness, activity in many ways being similar to running a business. This meant buying drugs as cheaply as possible and then trying to sell them on to make maximum profit, and this chapter examines how The Boys would do so. The Boys consumed drugs, but a lot of the time what they used themselves differed from what they sold and this chapter examines why this was the case. Many of the young men in the study also drank alcohol frequently, with some of them drinking heavily and often. I examine the challenges that drinking alcohol presented in a neighbourhood where most of the residents were Muslims.

Hustling is the only way to make money around here

Drug dealing was seen by The Boys as one of the only ways in which they were able to make quick money, and this would frequently come up in their conversations. Alam and Husband's study (2006) similarly highlighted how many young people in Bradford see drug dealing as an attractive career choice. One obvious explanation for involvement with drugs was because The Boys lived in a deprived neighbourhood and it is well documented that drug use (as well as drug dealing) has a close relationship with deprived neighbourhoods (Parker et al, 1988; Pearson, 2001). Pearson (2001: 53) found that: 'Where drugs such as heroin and crack-cocaine are concerned, the most serious concentrations of human difficulty are invariably found huddled together with unemployment, poverty, housing decay and other social disadvantages.'

One possible explanation for why drug dealing is an attractive line of work in deprived areas is because there are few legitimate avenues for success in these places (Kubrin, 2005). The inner city affords limited avenues for adolescents to obtain the types of social status and social roles available to youth in other environments (Rose, 1994). Given that ethnic minority individuals are much more likely to live in deprived areas (D. Smith, 2009: 34), they are, it is reported, much more likely to go on to hustle [drug deal] as a way in which to make money, and this, as Anderson (1994) noted in his study with black drug dealers, was because the opportunity for dealing drugs is literally just around the corner for them. In the same way it was easy for The Boys to become drug dealers. Some of the younger boys who were not yet established dealers would occasionally discuss the prospect of selling drugs to make quick money. One afternoon as we stood under a shop canopy sheltering from the rain, Yass and Ilyas started discussing which local dealers, from their perspective, had the best quality cannabis, and ruminated on the idea of buying a larger amount to then sell on in smaller amounts to make a profit:

Ilyas: "Let's buy a *danna* [ounce]. I know loads of *banda* [people] who will buy it off us. I'm telling you if the thing [cannabis] is good then we can make a nice raise [profit]."

Yass: "You're right. To be honest with you, I need to make some money to save up for a ride [car]. What else can we do? Work, but there's fuck all, plus who's gonna pay us a proper wage? I can't see that ever happening."

Jobs were seen as difficult to come by, and it is well documented that being from ethnic minority groups makes the task of finding employment even more difficult (Cross and Waldinger, 1997; Sandberg, 2008; Bucerius, 2014). Further to this, as mentioned in the previous chapter, jobs that were perceived as having the potential of affecting their status were considered unsuitable to undertake. Status and 'rep' [reputation] were crucial factors for survival on the streets; every effort would go into building these. Hustling [selling drugs] was seen by The Boys as a way they could make money, but also a way in which they could enhance their rep and credibility on the streets. This has previously been documented as an explanation of why youth become involved with drugs, seeking to not only make money but also build status among their peers (see also Adler, 1985; Jacobs, 1999; Bourgois, 2003). One way that this became evident was through selling more drugs than others, which would also often lead some to boast that they were selling more drugs than was in reality the case.

Boasting was common among The Boys

The Boys felt a need to try and impress each other and one way of doing this was through boasting. Boasting is recognised to be a common practice among youth on the streets who see material wealth as a form of status (Wilkinson, 2001). Similarly, Sandberg (2008: 614), in his ethnographic study with ethnic minority dealers in Norway, found that, 'In addition to accumulation of economic capital, dealing also augments street capital and gives "profit" in the form of honour or prestige in the street culture'. There was a very powerful element of competitiveness among The Boys, with each of them trying to outdo the others, which frequently led to them misrepresenting, or even outright lying to each other. Boasting took different forms, some would boast of how much money they could make, others would boast of how many contacts [dealers] they knew and how they could call on these if they ever needed anything. While we were sitting in Shah's girlfriend's flat one evening, The Boys were talking about some of their 'links' [usually used to refer to a drug dealer]. They were deliberating as to who among them had the best link, when Shah proudly told Ahmed of a potential link from whom he could buy heroin relatively cheaply:

> *Shah*: "Look my brother Ahmed, I know next man who's got some *maal* [heroin]. It's nine out of ten, its good stuff I'm telling you. He knows me well, see. I've looked after him in jail and he owes me a favour. Listen to me, phone him up and tell him that I gave you his number and, trust me, he will look after you, and the good thing is it's local for you, it's only up your road."

Ahmed, however, was not interested in what Shah had to say and made it known to him and to the others that he had his own links. Ahmed then told Shah of a particular individual who was so desperate to sell his drugs that he was ringing him constantly:

> *Ahmed*: "It's next man, he's trying to get me to buy off him. I've told him that I'm not interested, but he keeps phoning me. I'm not stupid, I know what he's trying to do, he wants me to buy a *danna* [ounce] off him for £585, and then he's gonna get it from next man for £500, and he makes a quick raise."

As illustrated previously, there were a lot of middlemen who would try to make money in the process of buying drugs from one dealer and then selling them onto another dealer for a slightly dearer price. Meanwhile boasting among The Boys was also done by talking of how they were able to get their hands on stolen goods, as was the case when Shaf was telling Ali one evening as we stood not far from where he lived how he was able to obtain the latest phones 'at near nothing':

> *Shaf:* "I was offered 100 iPhones the other day. This guy I
> know jacked a lorry and wanted to get shot of them quick.
> Let me know if anyone wants them. I'm even thinking
> 'bout getting the lot off him and then sell them. It could
> be a good little raise for me."

There were times when Shaf was not around that The Boys would have a laugh at his expense, recalling some of things he had previously lied about. Shaf had a reputation for making things up, and The Boys took whatever he told them with a pinch of salt. Ali: "He [Shaf] can make some right shit up: I don't know where he gets it all from. I'm sure he's losing the plot – he fucking believes his own lies."

Others in the neighbourhood were also known for boasting, but their boasts were seen as beyond belief and were therefore referred to instead as 'bullshitting'. When I met a friend of theirs called Jazy one day he was proud to make it known to me that he was a major drug dealer and how so many people from the neighbourhood wanted to buy drugs from him: "I got three different types of green [cannabis] on me, and my phone ain't stopped ringing all morning cuz loads of peeps want my thing, it's banging. It's ten out of ten, it's gonna be a day to make some money." [Laughs]

As we walked away from Jazy, Ahmed started laughing and later told me: "He makes me laugh. He's a 100 mile per hour and he chats some right shit. I swear he's the biggest bullshitter in Bradford."

It seemed that there was a fine line between boasting and outright 'bullshitting' and while it was acceptable to exaggerate events, to lie blatantly was not acceptable. However, such exaggeration by The Boys was almost charming in a delayed adolescence kind of way, but it also displayed a lack of judgement which was quite surprising. If any of The Boys were overheard by anyone observing them with a view to prosecution for drug dealing, then their boasts would be taken at face value and not as some immature braggadocio. If that were to be the case, then they would have created more severe problems for themselves than if they had said nothing at all or had simply acknowledged the truth of their own operations, which were after all (for the most part) quite small-scale. However, to be seen as a major drug dealer was seen as significant for enhancing status among their peers and boasting allowed some to present this image when in reality it was not always the case, as we will discuss further on in this chapter.

Selling drugs was like running a business

The principal motivation for The Boys, like so many others who are involved in drugs, was to make money and for that reason, drug dealing was conducted in many ways similar to running a business. In order to make a profit, one had to know the market; one had to know where one could buy the cheapest and best quality drugs. One then had to market the products, realising that there was competition from other drug dealers in the neighbourhood. Sandberg (2008) highlights this point in his study by stating that to be a successful drug dealer requires skills and competences which are very similar to those of running a business. In their thinking about drugs, The Boys frequently exhibited shrewd commercial and business qualities which, had they been applied to the supply and retail of a product such as vacuum cleaners, would have aroused admiration from others. The fact that their product was illegal can and often did blind people to the creative skills that they exhibited.

During the second year of the fieldwork, The Boys were constantly talking about a 'drought', an occasion when there was a lack of drugs available on the market which, as a result, had pushed prices up. Droughts in the drug market (as The Boys explained) occurred frequently. During this period Jameel was kicking himself one day, annoyed that he had missed out on a money-making opportunity:

> *Jameel*: "I could have got it [drugs] on tick [credit] if I wanted off next man, but nah I didn't bother, I thought forget it. I didn't know there'd be drought a week later. If I got them off him, trust me, I would have kept them back until prices were sky high and made a sick killing [considerable money]."

Since supply was unpredictable, The Boys often had to show inventiveness and enterprise in finding out what was available, and marketing that. There was, therefore, considerable flexibility among the group in switching from drug to drug to sell, depending on which was most easily available and which was selling well. In his study 'Black drug dealers in a white welfare state', Sandberg (2008) also found that drug markets are fluid and are constantly changing, with people moving in and out of the trade and up and down the market. In legitimate lines of business, this ability to respond to the laws of supply and demand would be seen as highly admirable as it clearly took considerable skill to be able to accomplish this successfully – which The Boys demonstrated. The Boys generally sold drugs such as heroin, crack cocaine and cannabis, although some now saw heroin as no longer having the demand – or profit-making potential – it once had. Therefore, there were some who like Ahmed would contemplate selling cannabis, aware that there was a growing cannabis market today in their neighbourhood and more importantly aware that the sentences given out by the courts to cannabis dealers are not as lengthy as those given out to heroin and crack dealers. One evening as we were in the car, Ahmed was singing along to a song by the rapper Tupac when someone they knew flashed them in his car so to acknowledge them. This individual was a friend of theirs, and, according to The Boys, he was making 'sick paper' [a lot of money] through selling cannabis. The Boys were impressed by his expensive sports car, and this left some feeling that they too ought to start selling cannabis, but they were also aware that trying to get their hands on quality cannabis could be difficult and that there was tough competition in that market.

All about making money

The offending behaviour of The Boys entailed a great emphasis on monetary gain. There were some who, like Bash, even felt that instead of having offended like they did in the past (which was usually out of sheer boredom or seeking a thrill), they should have put more of their efforts into trying to make money.

> *Bash:* "If I didn't go on so many benders [get drunk or be on drugs] and fuck around on the streets and, spent more time hustling [drug dealing], then I would be a made man today. I knew peeps [people] in Manchester, Leeds, everywhere. I could have had banging *maal* [drugs] in and sold it in no time but no, I used to like going on benders and that."

This sense of regret was certainly because, like all young people who reach adulthood, there was an expectation to provide for themselves and even in some cases for their families. There was also a sense that The Boys felt that the earlier in their career they started selling drugs then the more established they would be today and this was compounded by the fact that status within the group included the appearance of being able to hold one's own financially. The more money that one was able to make illegally would mean the higher one's status among one's peers. This reinforced competition among The Boys, who would at times compete with one another as to who had the most money. Levels of wealth it seemed were a means of also manipulating others, and even at times of belittling them. This was certainly the case of Shaf, who would make sure that the other Boys knew that he had more money than they did, reinforcing a sense of hierarchy within the group. There was one particular occasion when Shaf and Tanny started arguing. Shaf, who was drinking alcohol, started yelling at Tanny: "You're a fucking nobody. Who's got more money, me or you? You're fuck all, you ain't got a proper ride [nice car], and look how old you are."

This was typical behaviour for Shaf who when sober was quiet but when drunk would become violently aggressive, randomly seeking confrontations with anyone over anything.

Meanwhile, The Boys were almost always on the lookout for ways in which they could make money. In the second year of the study, while hanging out, as we so often did, we were eating food in a local takeaway. The Boys were deliberating as to which car they thought was better – an Audi R8, which was parked immediately outside the takeaway, or a Porsche that Jameel's friend owned and which he would occasionally borrow – when someone who Shaf knew walked in. The individual saw Shaf and came over to talk with him. Although no one other than Shaf appeared to know this particular person, he shook hands with all of us – it was customary among The Boys, and is among Pakistani men in general, to shake hands with one another on meeting. Shaf introduced him to The Boys, and then the conversation moved onto drugs from almost nowhere, with the individual in question asking Shaf if he knew anyone who was selling good quality cocaine. Shaf's response was:

> "Yeah bro, I know loads of peeps [people] with good thing. You should have come to me, and I would have got it for you. Well, you got my number now: put my digits [phone number] in your phone and next time you need it give me a tinkle [call]. I swear it will be a good thing, none of this bashed-up crap. Just give me a call, yeah?"

Shaf was quick to have spotted a money-making opportunity, and he, like so many of the others, was not the type to let such an opportunity go. For him it was a matter of a few phone calls, arranging to buy drugs from one person and giving them to another for a slightly dearer price. Shaf was proud that he could make money from being a middleman, often boasting that he was able to do it in a such a way that he would not have to 'get his hands dirty' [touch the drugs]: "I used to make a grand a week before and I never even used to touch anything. I used to get next mans to run around for me and all I used to do was sit in one place and count the paper [money]."

There appeared to be a lot of middlemen (or go-betweens) among The Boys, who, in the process, would try and make some money for themselves. This could be done by buying drugs from one person and then selling them to another, for a slightly higher price. Those of The Boys who were shrewd enough, as was the case with Shaf, were able to move drugs around without even having to touch them, be this by asking some of the younger boys to deliver them or by arranging for the customer to pick them up from somewhere they placed them.

The desire to live lavish lifestyles

The Boys aspired to live lavish lifestyles, wanting to drive expensive sports cars, own the latest phones and wear expensive clothes and jewellery (watches, necklaces). One reason for this was because they were aware that by doing so this would enhance their standing among their peers. Similarly previous research with young male offenders has highlighted how they feel a need to live lavish lifestyles (Cusson, 1983; Willis, 1990). Ali hoped to make enough money from hustling to buy a new car. Bash was driving an old car, one which had been damaged, and he too would often talk of how he planned to buy a new sports car:

Ali: "I'm buying a nice ride soon, probably Golf, R32."
Bash: "Nah, you should get something else, bro. I'm thinking of getting one of those, I told you before, you muppet. Why don't you just get an A4 or summat [something]?"

While The Boys would regularly talk about buying new cars, this never transpired, but talking about it was one way of demonstrating to the others that they had the money to do so, even if this was not the case. The materialism of The Boys also led to them being easily impressed by conspicuous consumption, though some of them were astute enough to wonder how their peers had been able to buy expensive goods, such as a £14,000 car.

Jameel: "I didn't think he had that sort of paper [money], but he's done all right for himself now. Got to say he's pulled, got a sick [nice] RS4 [an expensive Audi car]. Bet you anything, he's gonna kit it out and get it ready for the summer."

Ali: "Yeah, he's a show off, he's just bought it to show mans that he's doing well."

A further ostentatious manifestation of wealth (or trying to impress others) was the custom of hiring cars, which were incredibly expensive. There was an occasion when Jameel, Shaf and Ali hired a car for the weekend. It was a high-performance sports car, one that they could clearly not afford to buy, so for them the nearest thing to owning one was hiring it for a few days. However, only having the car for the weekend meant getting the most out of it – it was no good it being parked as it was necessary to be seen in it by as many youths from the neighbourhood as possible.

Cruising around in a car with a powerful engine was not cheap, which meant having to think of a way to obtain fuel. One evening as we sat in the car, Jameel asked Ali if he's got the 'plates', to which Ali replied: "Nah, they not in my car, they're in Ahmed's car." Jameel then phoned Ahmed asking him to bring the plates. A short while later Ahmed turned up, parked his car parallel and handed over two car registration plates to Ali through the car window. The Boys then hurriedly got out and changed the registration plates on the hired car with the ones that Ahmed had just handed them. They then drove to a petrol station, one which was a few miles away from their neighbourhood. Once at the petrol station, Ali, who was sitting in the passenger seat, got out and filled the car up with a full tank of fuel before calmly getting back into the car, at which point Jameel, without paying for the fuel, drove away. As The Boys drove off, they laughed gleefully because the person working in the petrol station did not even notice that they had driven off without paying for the fuel. It was surprising to see just how calm The Boys were when doing what they referred to as 'a petrol legger'. They seemed to enjoy the thrill of driving off without paying for the fuel, and perceived it as an amusing prank – which also had a monetary reward.

At times broke, no money

Although The Boys were far from rich, throwing money around and paying for others was a key element of keeping face. It was the sociocultural norm that if food (when eating out) was bought then one person would share his money with others, buying for them all. Failure to do so meant loss of face and humiliation. Anyone unable to pay for others would (as in the case of Afzal) avoid their company while he was broke. The Boys would often comment on how Afzal would only hang out with them when he had 'paper' [money] in his pocket.

While it was common for The Boys to come across as if they had a lot of money, there were times when some of them were clearly struggling financially. Their lifestyle meant that they had large amounts of money one day and none the next, but had no sense of needing to save or invest. There was an occasion when The Boys were sat in Bash's flat and they noticed that Kamran appeared not to be his usual self. He seemed down and dismayed, and it was obvious that something was bothering him. Ali asked him what was wrong, and, despite initially hesitating, Kamran responded. He told The Boys that he had fallen into considerable debt with people who he ticked [bought on credit] drugs from, and was now finding it difficult to pay them back. Unlike in the past when Kamran would boast of how he was making money, his situation was different now, and he was struggling to make ends meet. According to the others, this was because of the time Kamran had lost in prison, which meant that he was trying to work harder to catch up with some of the other more established drug dealers who were firmly set in their ways, but he was finding it difficult. Kamran was also not getting on with his family, finding himself involved in constant arguments; he wanted to move out of his parents' home but not having the money to do so meant that, for now, he had to stay put in what was a hostile environment:

> *Kamran*: "I can't live with them [family] no more. Need to make money so that I can get my own place, cuz to be honest, I can't be assed with them [parents]. They fucking twisted. One minute they're telling me I'm right and then they fucking siding with him [younger brother], plus I don't want to live round here anyway. There's too many nosy fuckers around here, they all want to know what you're doing and I don't trust any of 'em."

A few days earlier Kamran had been involved in a confrontation with youths from the area. He spoke of not getting on with a few individuals, and was convinced that they were reporting his criminal activities to the police. It is interesting to note that while the offending behaviour of The Boys was generally much more thoughtful these days, revolving to a great extent around financial reward, there nevertheless were times when it was spontaneous and impulsive, particularly when it came to violence.

There's far too much competition in the drug market

While drug dealing was seen to be a profitable business, some of The Boys felt that the considerable competition in the local drug market had made it difficult to make money. Therefore in order to beat off competition The Boys had to make certain lifestyle adjustments, including the hours of business that they kept, and when and where they would, so to speak, open shop. As The Boys were aware that heroin and crack addicts were keen to 'score' [buy drugs] first thing in the morning, some of The Boys who sold these drugs realised that in order to make money and beat the competition they would have to wake up early.

During the first year of the fieldwork, I was getting to grips with how The Boys lived, and at that point I had quickly learned that it was normal for most of The Boys to sleep well past midday, preferring to socialise in the late afternoon or in the evenings. It was at this stage that I would occasionally go for a walk around the neighbourhood or in the local park, as waking up early was something that I had been used to. One particular morning as I was walking along I saw Nav with Ahmed. They were both sitting in their cars and appeared to be waiting for someone. It was strange seeing any of The Boys up so early in the morning, as it was not yet 9 am. I stopped to talk with them, and felt that I had to ask them what they were doing so early in the morning, to which Nav replied quite openly that they were waiting for customers:

> Nav: "We got dps [drug deals drop-offs] to make, got *banda* [people] waiting. Thing is you can't be sleeping as gotta make paper [money], and you see the early morning is the best time to make it cuz that's when the smack-heads [drug addicts] are up and have cashed their giros and need to score [buy drugs]."

According to The Boys, the reason why there was fierce competition in the heroin and crack market today was because there were far fewer heroin and crack addicts living in Manningham compared to a number of years ago. Those of The Boys who had been selling drugs for longer remembered Manningham as being a hotspot for heroin and crack addicts:

> *Ahmed*: "There's no money left in drugs, there's too many dealers out there. You know, back in the days there used to be loads of smack-heads and only a few dealers in each area, but fuck me, today there's loads of dealers. But I still think there's money to be made selling skunk [skunkweed, a potent variety of cannabis] though, cuz everyone's smoking the shit, but the problem is it's hard to get good quality skunk for a good price."

Similarly for Ali, Bradford had more dealers than drug addicts today; in other words there was more supply than demand:

> *Ali*: "In most other cities there're loads of junkies, and they wait ages for their dealers to pull up in the street. Sometimes there's a queue of them waiting to buy drugs, but here it's the other way round. You've got drug dealers who go looking for junkies [drug addicts]. I met a guy the other day; he uses crack and he showed me a big list of numbers he had for so many different drug dealers."

According to Salman, there were so many dealers in Bradford because the process of setting up as a drug dealer was simple. He explained how one did not need a big investment and that there were considerable numbers of youths in the neighbourhood who looked up to older dealers, thinking that they too would make big money: "You see, every Tom, Dick and Harry around here wants to be a dealer. You got people thinking they're something special because they sell *puria* [small bags of heroin]."

In The Boys' perception it was easy to learn about drugs. They recalled when they themselves were younger and would hang around on the streets watching older dealers go about their business. Once they became familiar with the process, many took it up as a way to make money. Similarly, Hoffer (2006) found in his study that the skills his dealers attained were through a socialisation process on the streets. Another striking difference in the heroin and crack market in Manningham today was the clientele, with an increase in the number from the Pakistani community who were using heroin. Whereas in the past the majority of heroin addicts in the neighbourhood were, according to The Boys, white, today there was an increasing number of *apnas* [Pakistanis] who were using heroin. Jameel: "Back in them days there used to be loads of *goras* [white people] on it, but what you see now is loads of *apnas* [Pakistanis] on *maal* [heroin]. You even got *apnania* [Pakistani girls] on it."

As the comment made by Jameel highlights, The Boys felt that the majority of the heroin addicts (who once were white residents) no longer lived in their neighbourhood, and this, as mentioned in Chapter Two was largely because of 'white flight'. Some of The Boys would speak of a time when there were more addicts living in certain parts of their neighbourhood. Ahmed: "There used to be loads of 'em down death row, Lumb Lane flats, but there's only a few here and there now."

On another occasion, Ali mentioned how in the past some British Pakistani dealers would refuse to sell heroin to fellow Pakistanis in fear of reprisals from family members, but that this has changed today:

> *Ali*: "Back in the days, there were only one or two *apnas* [Pakistanis] on *maal* [heroin]. There were some *apna* [Pakistani] dealers who wouldn't sell to 'em cuz they knew their family and, like, used to feel for 'em, but things are different now. Now you got dealers around here who only sell to *apnas* [Pakistanis – also translated as 'own people'] cuz there's loads of 'em on *maal*. And the other thing is that when you sell to people you know, there's less chance getting caught."

The explanation behind why some Pakistani drug dealers choose to only sell drugs to *apnas* was because, as highlighted by Ali's comment, this carried with it less risk of being exposed to the police. Those who one knew and trusted were less likely to report their activities to the police, and they were able to deal in drugs without raising suspicions, as it was difficult for the police to detect whether they were friends or whether one of them was selling drugs to the other.

The Boys were shrewd when hustling

The Boys were shrewd when it came to drug dealing, constantly trying to avoid detection by the police, and usually going about their business in cars, dropping drugs off to waiting customers. Generally speaking, The Boys only sold drugs to people whom they knew and trusted. The Kids who hustled generally did so while hanging around on the streets, and sold in what was known as 'smaller deals'. Some of The Kids even sold for The Boys, others would have drugs on tick. This was the case with Yass, who at one stage was getting his drugs from Ali, who was giving it to him on tick [credit]. This only became apparent when I was with The Boys one evening and they stopped their car to speak with some of The Kids who were hanging around near the shops. Ali put down his window and asked Yass when he was paying him his money, to which Yass replied: "Give me 'bout a week, bro, it's going proper slow. The thing [drugs] weren't all that – I gave it to some of my regulars and they like this is proper shit, give us our money back."

Yass was on this occasion struggling to sell the drugs he had off Ali as the quality was not as good as previously, which made it more difficult to sell to his customers. Meanwhile, those of The Boys who sold drugs appeared to work individually rather than collectively, although it did seem that Ali and Bash were in some kind of partnership, but this was difficult to verify. There were times when they would disappear and reappear without explanation. The most probable explanation was that, by going missing like this they facilitated deals they wished to finalise, but this has to be inferred because it was not observed, and was, therefore, unable to be proved. Having said that, there was an occasion when I accompanied Ali and Bash to what I later learned was a trip to see the quality of drugs that another dealer was selling. As The Boys parked their car in a cul-de-sac, Bash made a phone call to someone informing them that he had arrived. Several minutes later a car pulled up, and in it were two men of similar age. Bash and Ali went to sit in the other car. After a short while, they headed back to their own vehicle and we drove off. On the way back Ali and Bash discussed what their thoughts were on the quality of the drugs that they had just seen:

Ali:	"It looked TT [ten out of ten] to me but got to get someone to try it to see what it really is like."
Bash:	"Yeah, well, get a tester off him next time. He says he can get loads of it anyway, I don't know if he can though!"
Ali:	He don't look like the type who chats shit. He looks all right to me, he wasn't bragging about anything so seemed all right."

The Boys then deliberated about the amount they would buy and when they would be able to get the money together. Two qualities characterised the deals The Boys made in their acquisitions. First, they had to ensure the quality of the drugs they were buying and, second, they had to be sure that the people they were dealing with were not undercover police, or people who would arrange a later meeting where large amounts of money would be exchanged only to rob them (see 'Ripps' section, later).

There were no obvious ways of ascertaining quality short of trying out the drugs. Much decision making was based on experience and gut instinct. Similar problems also affected their assessment of whom it was safe to sell to. A prominent difference among The Boys and The Kids in their hustling was how much more cautious The Boys were in comparison with The Kids when going about selling drugs. The Boys, it appeared, generally only sold drugs in what was known as 'closed market', relying on the mobile phone to make deals (May and Hough, 2004) and, again, only selling to people whom they knew and trusted. One evening Bash was boasting to the others how some of his customers were professionals, and that he would refuse to sell to anyone he did not know, just in case they were undercover police officers:

> *Bash*: "I only sell to people who got jobs and who look after themselves. I got good customers. I got a probation officer who buys off me. I'm telling you if you looked at him you wouldn't even think that this man is on *maal* [heroin]. I ain't stupid, I'm not gonna sell to the scruffy junkies [addicts] – you're fucking asking to get locked up if you sell to them. Five-O [police] are always on their case, all they got to do is follow them and when they meet to score off you, they bust you."

The Boys were aware that if they were arrested and charged for supplying drugs then they risked going to prison for significant time. Prison could mean that they would lose the customers they had and they were also aware that they would find it difficult to try and build clientele on their release from custody as other dealers were quick to replace them. One way to avoid detection was to sell only to those individuals who they trusted, but for some of The Kids the desire to make quick money would see them take considerable risks. This was partly because The Kids were not yet established drug dealers, and felt a need to find new customers in order to increase their profits. I observed some of The Kids searching for new clients, standing around on the street corners and trying to identify potential customers walking past. However, this also presented a danger that the police could relatively easily detect them, as visibility is considered to be the markets greatest disadvantage (May and Hough, 2004). The Boys viewed the police as deliberately targeting Pakistani street dealers while turning a blind eye to those of other backgrounds.

The police love stitching us up

The Boys would discuss many a time during the study how, in their view, the police would dupe local youth by posing as junkies [drug addicts]. Previous research has highlighted how the police are known to pose as drug addicts in some neighbourhoods in order to establish who the drug dealers are (Hay, 2005). However, this was something that The Boys found troubling as they felt that the police were deliberately targeting men from their ethnicity. One evening as we sat in the car, The Boys were laughing at what they considered was sheer stupidity by one of The Kids who had been arrested for selling heroin to the same undercover police officer on more than one occasion. While The Boys found this to be amusing, at the same time they were furious with the tactics that were used by the police. In fact, some of The Boys were blaming the police outright for deliberately going out and enticing Pakistani youth into selling drugs to them. Shaf, who was drinking alcohol at the time, made it known what he thought:

Shaf: "The police jus' love stitching up people, they ain't fucking stupid. Don't tell me they don't know that some of these lot [younger boys] aren't even, like, proper dealers."

Nav: "You're right, bro. I bet you anything if a smack-head [addict] came to anyone around here and wanted to buy drugs, they [youth] would say to them 'yeah, I can get you it', and then they will phone around and try and make money, but the thing is that doesn't make you a dealer. That's fucking anyone seeing like an opportunity to make a bit of money."

There was a perception among The Boys that some of the local youth would do anything to make money. Even those who were not, in their view, 'proper' dealers would not let opportunities to make money pass them by. A person did not even need to know a great deal about how the drug-dealing business worked, for all he needed to know was that there was a potential customer who wanted drugs, and that he was able to get them for him from someone else. Salman spoke one day of how the younger lot did not, in his view, have a clue what they were doing at times:

> *Salman*: "You see, like, the boys on the streets and they ain't got a clue what they're doing or owt [anything], they take stupid risks. Some of them are going up to people they don't even know, and who they think are smack-heads [addicts], asking them if they want to buy *maal* [heroin]."

The ability to identify plain-clothes police is a fundamental aspect for street dealers (Johnson and Natarajan, 1995; Jacobs, 1996, 1999). However, the above incident highlights the inexperience of some of the young Pakistani dealers who aspire to make money from drugs but who are, a lot of the time, unable to detect undercover police among their genuine customers. On another occasion while we were cruising Ahmed stopped the car and went into the shop to buy the *Telegraph and Argus*, the local newspaper. In it he saw someone from the area whom he knew who had been caught by the police with a substantial amount of drugs and had been sentenced to a lengthy spell in prison. Ahmed informed Ali and Jameel about the length of his sentence, and they all appeared stunned, with Nav shouting: "What the fuck, can't believe that. He didn't even have a clue what he was doing. He weren't a fucking dealer. That's bullshit."

According to The Boys the individual concerned was working for someone else and, despite him having been in possession of the drugs, he was according to The Boys not the dealer. There was a feeling among The Boys that the police often knew that the younger boys worked for older dealers but felt that they were not interested in that fact. This was a real issue for Bash, who was convinced that the police rarely took out the major dealers in Bradford:

> *Bash*: "*Mawe* [police] just try and do any mans over. They know that some of these lads ain't proper dealers but for them it's not about that, it's 'bout getting a promotion and making out that they've just taken out Mr Big, when they just take out people who ain't got a clue what they're doing and who get used by peeps [bigger dealers]."

The value system of the younger generation as mentioned previously was that to be associated with drug dealing and older established dealers was a badge of honour. However, what emerged from the above observation was the way in which dealing perpetuates itself. There was, at the same time, a feeling among some of The Kids that because they were younger and did not drive around in cars like The Boys, they were not suspected of being drug dealers by the police. This was illustrated when we cruising with The Boys, we saw some of The Kids standing near Zaks. Wahid who was standing by the car was counting a small bundle of £10 notes, and was annoyed that he had lost money, telling the others, "I've lost some money out of me pocket, I don't know where it's gone." Salman, who knew how Wahid was making money, told him, "Be careful, you don't want to get banged up." He was implying to Wahid that he should be vigilant so that he was not caught by the police. However, Wahid replied confidently to Salman: "I'm always careful. The thing is, I'm always on foot walking around, and this way nobody even thinks I'm doing owt [anything] dodgy."

Wahid then proudly pointed his finger to a car with two men sitting in it and told Salman that they had just 'scored off him' [purchased drugs from him]. As The Boys were aware of the sentences handed down to drug dealers by the courts, they reinforced the need for The Kids to be cautious when going about their hustling, aware that getting caught and 'doing time' was never far away from 'the game' [selling drugs].

The Boys also felt that sentences that were often given to British Pakistani dealers were far too long for the crime they committed. One reason for this feeling was that The Boys were able to put themselves in the shoes of other dealers and felt sympathy for them. This sense of sympathy was not surprising: all of The Boys were aware that what had happened to others could happen to them. There was a sense of fellow-feeling and of solidarity with rivals who were caught and punished. At the same time, there was a sense of disproportion in that long sentences for some drugs seemed to them to be inappropriate as, in their eyes, many of the drugs they sold were simply trivial in the scale of offences. The Boys did have a sense of moral vision, and the inconsistencies of the law over drugs often made sentencing seem unfair.

Ripps were less risk then hustling

Another method of making money, and one which was related closely with drug dealing was involvement in *ripps*. *Ripps*, according to The Boys, was when they took something off someone without paying for it, and did so in a somewhat blatant manner. Examples of *ripps* included arranging to buy drugs but taking them without paying for them or arranging to sell drugs to someone but instead of giving them the drugs, robbing them of their money. Previous research has highlighted how drug dealers often steal and use violence on one another and which most of the time goes unnoticed by the criminal justice system (Topalli and Wright, 2002). Among The Boys there was almost always discussion of someone in the neighbourhood having been *ripped* or having *ripped* someone else. One evening as we were sitting in Bash's flat, The Boys were talking about a *ripp* that a local dealer had carried out on another dealer, and this led to Salman and Kamran recalling how they themselves had previously *ripped* someone who they arranged to sell drugs to:

> *Salman*: "It was proper funny, *kasmay* [honestly]. Man came all the way from Baildon. I knew him cuz he used to buy off me now and then, but this time round Kamran's, like, 'Don't give him the *maal* [heroin], let's rip him'. To be honest with ya, I didn't even want to do it, I knew I'd lose a good customer, but then I thought fuck it, he was a mug [fool] anyway, so I said to him, I've got the thing [drugs] on me, and he pulled out the paper [money]. Kamran, the fucker, grabbed it and shot off [ran away], so I said to him, 'Don't fucking look at me, he's got the thing' and I just chipped [ran] as well. He followed us up the road; the poor bastard was begging us. He was shouting at us saying it was his dad's money but he was just chatting it [speaking nonsense]. How the fuck could it have been his dad's money?"

It was evident that being involved in *ripps* gave The Boys credibility which could then be bragged about, telling others how the *ripp* had been conducted. However, although *ripps* could be considered as robbing someone, to The Boys they were very much different because, unlike when one carried out a robbery and the individual who has been robbed then reports the robbery to the police, *ripps* in the eyes of The Boys carried with them less risk as the police rarely knew what went on. Ahmed explained on another occasion how for this reason he felt that ripps were 'safer': "Doing ripps are safer cuz there's less of a chance of getting caught. No one that has been ripped will call the police and say that my dealer's just robbed my money cuz he knows the police will say to him, what were you doing buying drugs?" [Laughs]

Carrying out *ripps* could sometimes see weapons used in the process and some of The Boys would often discuss how they themselves had previously used weapons when conducting *ripps*. While I was hanging out one afternoon with Bash and Ali, we were in town and ended up in a shop which, as well as other items, sold replica guns. Bash and Ali started looking closely at a particular replica gun and commented on how it looked like 'the real thing'. Bash then decided to hold it, and shouted over to Ali: "It looks the thing. Look at it, it even weighs the same, bro, hold it."

Ali and Bash then start discussing how they could use a replica gun when carrying out a *ripp*. However, this did not necessarily mean anything, as it was incredibly common for The Boys to talk about things and not carry them out; in fact this was something I became familiar with early on in the study. But if Bash and Ali did carry out the *ripp* then they did a great job in keeping it secret – I was with The Boys for the next few weeks, and there was no further conversation about the planned *ripp*, so I presumed it was once again only small talk. Some of The Kids were also involved in *ripps*, but these were, most of the time, less confrontational. In the third year of the study Ilyas was telling the others one day how he had *ripped* someone, having taken a dealer's drugs from where he hid them:

> *Ilyas*: "I saw next man [drug dealer] walking up the alley and I knew he was up to summat [something] cuz he looked proper suspicious. He kept looking back to see if I was looking at him or not. I knew he was up to something dodgy, so when he chipped [went away], I went to where he was and I looked, like, closely and I saw some foil wrapped in a see-through bag. I thought to myself what's this? I looked in it and there were some *puraih* [small deals of heroin] so I took them." [Laughs]

Drugs could not be stored at their homes in case the police were to search them, so most of The Boys who sold drugs would store them in various locations, but at the same time they were aware that their drug stashes could go missing. Therefore, it was important to ensure that no one else knew where one kept their drugs overnight, and for this reason there was a great degree of secrecy in this matter even among The Boys.

Far from being 'Mr Bigs'

When one looks more closely at the young men in the study and their drug dealing, one quickly apprehends that they were, in reality, far from what one would consider major dealers in the drugs business. While some from among The Boys could have easily convinced people that they were major dealers and could get their hands on considerable drugs, this was far from being the case. The Boys, generally only supplied it in small amounts, and while the authorities (and even some of the elders) in the community perceived them to be major dealers, those who know the drug–dealing business will be very aware that, contrary to the widely held beliefs of the police and judiciary, selling small quantities of drugs does not make one a major drug dealer. The Boys were small-scale dealers who themselves aspired to become bigger dealers. There were as discussed earlier other reasons why being perceived as a major drug dealer was appealing to The Boys. Selling considerable amounts of drugs enhanced status among their peers and this, combined with being seen by one's peers driving expensive cars and wearing expensive clothes, contributed to enhancing one's credibility on the streets. In the view of The Boys, having credibility was paramount. While sitting in the car one day, Shaf explained how it was not always the amount of money one had that helped enhance his credibility:

> *Shaf:* "You see, having a rep is what you need around here, and when you're a shotter [a dealer] you can make this, cuz this way then you're seen as someone who no one dare fucks with. Cuz they know that man's gonna be connected, as he's in that sort of game where he's defo knows peeps [people] and get you dealt with."

Here Shaf is acknowledging that the commercial aspect of trafficking in drugs was only a fraction of the issue. Rep [reputation, credibility] was closely linked to involvement in drugs, and this in turn is, in part, based on whom one was associated with – who one's contacts were and, concomitantly, how ruthless one is perceived to be in terms of drug dealing, and association with other ruthless people. Ruthlessness earns respect, while gentleness, consideration and kindness were perceived as weaknesses to be at best scorned and at worst abused. Fagan and Wilkinson (1998) have highlighted in their study that young inner-city males take reputation seriously and try hard to gain respect from peers. As drug dealers conduct their business outside the realms of police protection, it is seen as necessary to build a reputation as being violent and aggressive, deterring others from attempting any future assault (Jacobs, 1999). Therefore the need to appear a 'big player' and to boast in order to get respect and status from others would lead to small-time dealers masquerading as major dealers and hardened big-time gangsters – as if the minnow wanted to be taken for the shark. This, however, was often counterproductive as it would also mean that the courts would view their image management at face value, and often give sentences which The Boys regarded as out of proportion to the reality of their activities, notwithstanding their posing. This led to an interesting situation for The Boys. They were aware that they risked prison, and that prison would have a permanent and negative effect on their lives because a prison record would effectively bar them from legitimate employment. They were also aware that prison sentences could often be lengthy and, in their eyes, disproportionate to the nature of their crime, yet they persisted in this risk-taking behaviour. They often regarded the lads who got caught as incompetent operators, or, in the words of Yass describing Wahid when he got caught, "a dopey fucker". This overconfident assumption that it wouldn't happen to them characterised many of The Boys. The discussion so far in this chapter has been around involvement in drug dealing; the young men in the study also consumed a number of drugs as well as alcohol and we discuss their drug habits and alcohol consumption next.

Drug use among The Boys

The Boys used a number of drugs but, having said this, their attitude towards the consumption of drugs appeared to have changed as they had grown older. When younger, they spoke of having taken more of a wildly hedonistic and self-indulgent approach, but with age there came a greater willingness to consume in a controlled way, using expertise to replace the indiscriminate enthusiasm typical of overeager but under-discerning youngsters. Research has also highlighted how drug habits change with age (Boys, Marsden and Strang, 2001). Some of The Boys spoke of how when they were younger they would use anything that gave them a 'buzz'. There was, according to The Boys, one particular drug which they no longer used but which they used regularly when they were younger:

> *Salman*: "Sometimes we'd get them [Ecstasy] and see who could take the most tablets, we used to be like proper mad ones. I remember one time we couldn't get them and we phoned everyone, no one had anything on them then so we asked one of the boys and he said he could get them from Keighley. So we all went on the bus and got them."

Another explanation for their controlled drugs use was that there was a sense that drug habits had the potential of damaging street credibility (Sandberg, 2008), as sustained exposure to specific drugs impaired powers of reasoning, and risked turning them into men who were unable to think straight and therefore to cope. There was a growing and belated realisation that certain drugs created the conditions for mental health problems later in life. This may be seen by others as 'shutting the stable door after the horse has bolted', but it was the dawning of this understanding of what drugs were in danger of doing to them that led some of The Boys to cease using some drugs themselves, although the profit motive in supplying these same drugs to others remained undimmed. The motivation for many of The Boys involved in selling drugs was to make money, and they were astute enough to realise that if they consumed their own product they were unlikely to make much money and were likely to develop a dependency which would be self-defeating. Therefore, many of The Boys held in their minds a sharp differentiation between selling to others and using what they sold.

There was also a reluctance to try out new drugs now, particularly those they knew little about. This was to become apparent when one evening as we sat in Bash's flat. Tosh, someone who lived nearby, was also there. He was no stranger: although he did not hang out with The Boys these days, he was nevertheless someone with whom The Boys had spent a lot of time. From his appearance, Tosh looked like a heavy drug user with dark eyes and rotting teeth, and my suspicions were later confirmed when The Boys informed me that he was "always off his head". Anyway, Tosh started talking to The Boys about a drug that, according to him, "loads of people were now using", and he wanted The Boys to think of the money they could make from selling it. He then took out of his pocket a small bag of cling film and opened it. In it was a white powdery substance. He placed it on the table in front of him and, using a bank card, broke down the substance and then snorted the powder up his nose using a rolled bank note. The Boys were familiar with the manner in which Tosh consumed the drug as it was the exact method in which some of them consumed cocaine. However, the difference on this occasion was that this powdery substance, although it looked very much like cocaine, was not cocaine but M-Kat. The Boys appeared intrigued, asking Tosh what it felt like when snorting it, but they were reluctant to try it themselves, even when Tosh tried to convince them:

Tosh: "It's good shit, not bad I swear, it's a bit like KoKa [cocaine]. I can get my hands on as much as you wanted, I can get hold of loads and we can make some right money on it. Try a bit bro, come on, try it."

85

Jameel: "I ain't smoking that shit, Tosh, it's a fucking killer, you ain't got a clue what's in it. I've heard it's mixed with all sorts of shit, you must think I'm crazy to snort that shit. I'm happy with KoKa [cocaine] – it's the real thing not some cheap bullshit thing."

However, for all their commercial skills, on this specific occasion, and perhaps unexpectedly, The Boys declined an opportunity which seemed potentially both profitable and pleasurable. Although drug consumption was more controlled these days, there were occasions during the study when some of The Boys would go on what they referred to as benders [bingeing]. These benders tended to only be on special occasions such as a wedding or Eid, or if it was one of their birthdays.

As well as consuming drugs, a number of The Boys drank *Sharaab* [alcohol]. It is important to highlight here that alcohol consumption was not a big deal when The Boys were by themselves and in private, only focusing on consumption of a substance that made them feel good. However, they found themselves in a difficult situation when wanting to drink, as alcohol consumption was considered *haraam* [forbidden] and The Boys lived in a community which consisted almost entirely of Muslim residents. This meant that, not only was it difficult when trying to purchase it, but finding a suitable place to drink was another dilemma. Drinking alcohol openly in their neighbourhood was unthinkable, with The Boys aware that their parents would be furious if they heard that they had been drinking.

It might seem that the solution for those of The Boys who did elect to drink alcohol was for them to go to a local pub, but this option was unrealistic. To be seen entering or leaving a pub would mean being known as a drinker in the community. This would risk family members learning of it, and risk stigma in a community which it appeared in some ways accepted hard drugs more readily than it accepted alcohol. To an outsider this raises a major problem in trying to understand the lives of The Boys, as it is seemingly all right to consume drugs which cause addiction, create psychological problems and cause major health problems because these are not specifically condemned by name in the Quran, whereas alcohol is condemned for the self-same reason. So The Boys would take drugs with no sense of ambivalence, but feel ambivalent when taking alcohol. There would at times be conversation among The Boys of how they would much rather sell drugs than be involved in the sale of alcohol, considering the sin of selling alcohol greater in their Islamic faith than selling drugs (see Chapter Six for further discussion). Alcohol caused The Boys to become involved in regular arguments among themselves. While cruising around in the car one evening with Ali, Shaf, Jameel and Tanny, they decided to get something to eat. They asked one another where they should go for food. Tanny suggested that we go to a particular place, as the food there was really nice, telling The Boys that he had been there with his dad a few days previously. On hearing this, Shaf who knew Tanny's family well, replied to Tanny in a hostile manner: "Why the fuck you lying? You don't even get on with your dad and you saying you went with him for food." Although Tanny would only hang out with The Boys occasionally, he nevertheless was not ready to be spoken to in this way. Tanny replied to Shaf: "Don't dare talk to me like a piece of shit, you shut the fuck up before I knock your fucking jaw off."

Tanny and Shaf started swearing at each other and became aggressive, and it was only because Shaf was sitting in the passenger seat and Tanny sat in the back behind the driver that they found it difficult to get at each other. Then, from nowhere, the conversation turned to money and Tanny's sisters. Shaf, who was clearly drunk, started shouting at Tanny.

> *Shaf*: "Who is worth more, me or you? I got a lot more money than you. What have you got, fuck all, eh? You're full of shit, Tanny. You can't even control your sisters; they go to shisha lounges [places to smoke a hookah]. If my sisters went there and didn't dress properly, I would deal with them."

Jameel and Ali were shocked with what Shaf was saying. To talk about one's sisters was something that The Boys refrained from doing, considering it to be extremely disrespectful to do so. This, however, also highlighted the point that in the eyes of The Boys seeing their sisters dress inappropriately or behave in a manner which was disrespectful could bring them considerable embarrassment. The Boys were seen as keeping their sisters in check and encouraging them to maintain the family *Izzat* [respect], although this raised the question of why they did not behave in the same way. However, such low digs from Shaf were clearly making Tanny extremely aggressive. He began shouting, "I'm gonna knock you the fuck out", as he leaned over me to get to Shaf. It was all getting out of control, and Ali, who was driving at the time, had little choice but to park the car in the middle of the road and, along with Jameel, try and calm the situation down: "What the fuck, you're like a fucking kid. I thought you two are meant to be good family friends. Even kids don't act like this." Ali, who was probably the closest to Shaf, looked at him and whispered to him: "You need to shut the fuck up or else you're gonna get hurt. If you can't control your drink, then don't fucking drink."

After numerous attempts to try and calm Tanny down, he eventually did, although he did not talk to Shaf for the rest of the evening. But then the following day Shaf apologised, blaming his behaviour and actions on alcohol. Shaf had a drink problem: he would rarely ever drink casually and would almost always get drunk. Previous research has highlighted how it is rare to hear of occasional drinkers among Muslims, as those who break the Quranic law are more likely to be binge drinkers or alcoholics (Orford et al, 2004; Bolognani, 2009). The group culture of The Boys was unsympathetic to emotional issues, so any individual who had any sort of emotional problem was unable to share these with The Boys, and this may well explain, in the case of Shaf, the way in which he seemed to take refuge in excessive consumption of alcohol, the impression being that he was, in some unacknowledged way, 'drowning his sorrows' because of some private and undisclosed source of distress.

During the latter part of the second year of the study Shaf's drinking problem got so bad that his parents persuaded him to go to Pakistan, in the hope that a trip to Pakistan would help him to stop drinking. His parents, according to The Boys, felt they needed to do something as they did not want everyone in the neighbourhood knowing that their son was an alcoholic. The logic behind such trips to Pakistan was that alcohol is illegal there and is much harder to obtain, so those who had drinking problems would find it easier to refrain. In addition, there were times when parents were known to send their children to Pakistan in order to help them with their drug addictions. The Boys explained that there were a number of people who they knew of who were now living in Pakistan because of heroin addictions.

Violence was impulsive

Despite the offending behaviours of The Boys changing with maturity, they continued to behave impulsively when it came to violence. Research has documented that there are a number of explanations of why young people behave violently. One is attributed to young people themselves having witnessed violence or having been affected by violent behaviour (Kitzmann et al, 2003; Sherrer, 2008; McGivern, 2010). Another is young people having traits which are more impulsive when compared with adults (Soller et al, 2014). Although The Boys did not go out deliberately looking to get into fights, their boisterous behaviour would sometimes offend others, and this would lead to confrontations and even at times physical fights.

There was an occasion during the study, as we were cruising in the car, when Ahmed became annoyed with the driver ahead who was driving much too slow for his liking. In trying to convince him to speed up, Ahmed decided to tailgate the car ahead, and the driver stuck two fingers up. This infuriated Ahmed so much so that he overtook the car dangerously, and then slammed on his brakes so that the other driver also had to stop. He then left his car at a standstill. The other driver, who was a white male in his late thirties, got out of his car and walked alongside Ahmed's car. On seeing him approaching in his mirror, Ahmed also got out. This led to a confrontation, with the driver aggressively asking Ahmed why he was tailgating him. Tensions quickly increased and both started raising their voices, at which point Ahmed started threatening to hit the other driver: "I'll fuck you up, you fucking prick. Don't give me the big one, you don't know me. I swear, I'll fuck you up, get out my face, you twat [idiot]." It was only when other cars behind started tooting their horns, eager for the traffic to move on, that Ahmed decided to get back into his car and drive off, aware that someone may have called the police and he could end up being arrested.

Confrontations among The Boys would often begin as a result of someone believing that someone else had stared at them for too long. Staring was seen as an act of aggression, even if the other person did not actually intend to stare. Any accusation of having stared would be met head-on with aggression. Previous research has also noted how 'dirty looks' (staring) can lead to violence among young people (Phillips, 2003). On one occasion while I was with Ali and Ahmed cruising through the town we saw Shah walking. The Boys stopped the car to offer him a lift. Once in the car, we noticed that Shah's eye was swollen, and when The Boys enquired about what had happened, he replied that he had been jumped [involved in a fight]. He explained that he had been walking when:

> Shah: "These apna [Pakistani] lads kept looking at me and then one of them said to me, 'What you looking at?', and I said 'Your fucking face!' And then next minute him and his friends all bounced on me. They thought they were bad men, I swear. I knew I couldn't take them all on, so all I did was cover my face and I just took the blows. You know I would have fucked them all up. The bastards couldn't even

punch, they punched like women. Not to worry though, I will see them again."

Several features emerged from Shah's comment. One was the sense of having to respond with aggression even if the original aggressive remark was wide of the mark, so that hostility begets hostility. A second factor was the sense of safety in numbers; a group were prepared to attack a single individual whereas in the past The Boys spoke of there being a greater likelihood of seeing that as unfair odds. But Shah's response was also revealing in that he now had a grievance he was nursing, and a vendetta had arisen which would be continued, the level of violence becoming self-perpetuating.

On a separate occasion in the third year of the study while hanging out with The Kids, Yass was proudly showing the others who stood around his swollen knuckles. He then told them what had happened when someone was staring at him:

> Yass: "You should have seen him, he was looking at me like he was someone special. It's cuz he had this gal [girlfriend] with him, so I said to him, 'What the fuck you giving me daggers for?' He starts giving the large one and giving me lip, so I just whacked him in his face. Should have seen him, and his gal was screaming all over the place, so I did one [ran off] before she phoned *mawe* [police]."

It was worrying to see The Boys involved in physical fights simply because someone stared at them for too long, or even looked at them in the wrong way. However, having said this, there were some people in the neighbourhood who considered it stupid to fight merely because someone looked at them for too long. This was to become evident when, in the gym one day with Ali, Salman and Bash, they got talking with someone they knew. The Boys had not seen this particular individual for some time and were pleased to see him, asking him where he had been, to which he told them that he had moved away from the local area. When asked why, he replied by telling them that:

> "There's too much tension around here, man. You just on edge all the time in case you say summat [something] to someone, they take it the wrong way and start fighting with you. You park your car at the lights and you don't even dare look to see who's in the car next to you, in case they turn around and say, 'What the fuck you looking at?' and then

you get into a fight – for what, for looking at someone? It's
bullshit. It's not what I want to be doing now. I don't want
to be fighting now, especially not for stupid fucking things."

As highlighted here, there were different perceptions on violence
among residents living in the neighbourhood. Some – particularly the
elders in the neighbourhood – saw it as immoral to physically hurt
anyone, whereas others, like The Boys and The Kids, saw violence as
a way in which to settle disputes.

Fighting 'one-on-one'

This section examines how violence would at times involve organised
fights taking place that The Boys referred to as 'one-on-one' fights.
These fights were often well organised by The Boys themselves or
their friends. Research has highlighted how some groups are known
to settle disputes in what can be termed bare-knuckle fighting (Currie,
2009). While cruising around in the car with Ali, Jameel and Bash one
day, The Boys received news of a fight that was about to take place
between two local lads. The fight was due to a drug debt. The thought
of seeing the two lads fight excited The Boys, and they were in a hurry
to reach the venue and witness it. As we drove down a back lane not
too far from where The Boys lived and onto a playing field, we saw
considerable numbers of other youths who had assembled to watch
the fight. The atmosphere was tense. Heated discussions took place
on both sides before the two individuals stepped forward and started
fighting. Considerable shouting could be heard from those watching,
spurring on the one they wanted to win. The fight itself was brutal,
but it did not go on for long, lasting only a few minutes before those
who were watching decided to split it up. The fight led to injury for
one of the lads whose nose was bloodied and appeared to be broken.
At this point rumours circulated that the police were on their way
which saw everyone quickly disperse.

On the way back from the fight, The Boys spoke at some length about
what had happened. They had expected the individual whom they
knew better to have destroyed [beat] the other, but, to their surprise,
this had not been the case. Bash was frantic, shouting as though he
was some kind of fight trainer: "I swear he should have just taken him
down and choked the fucker out." According to The Boys, fighting
toe-to-toe was not always wise, as they felt that in some cases it was
better to fight on the floor. Anyway, later that evening as The Boys all
got together, Umar and Bilal (two of the Marginal Boys) turned up at

Bash's flat after hearing about the fight, to find out more. Ali's response was to express regret that he had not recorded it on his mobile phone, and he was busy phoning around to find out if anyone who had seen it had recorded it. The Boys spoke at some length about the fight, and those who had watched it described as best they could, with Bash even trying to get Bilal in a 'rear naked choke', demonstrating what he would have done if it was him who had been fighting. Fighting to settle disputes was common, but some of The Boys spoke of preferring to use weapons rather than have to fight one-on-one.

Meanwhile, if any of The Boys was ever involved in a fight or a disagreement then it was expected that the others demonstrate their solidarity. Tanny and someone from another neighbourhood had argued, the argument having stemmed from a family disagreement over disputed land in Pakistan, which both families were now battling over. Tanny was now receiving threats from his cousin, and showed Salman the texts he had received, on which Salman decided to phone this individual and speak with him. The conversation quickly became heated, with Salman threatening to 'fuck him up' [beat him up], shouting over the phone to Tanny's cousin: "If you've drunk your mum's milk, then come and fight me." This bizarre and seemingly incoherent phrase was a challenge, saying to the rival that if he was his mother's child then he should not run scared. Consequently the two arranged to fight and Salman, Ali, Jameel and Ahmed went along to what they thought would be a fight between Salman and Tanny's cousin. However, the fight did not take place as the other individual's uncle managed to convince Salman and his nephew to sort the matter out verbally rather than by fighting.

The 'John Wayne' mentality of resolving disputes through fighting was a source of profound tribulation to the community elders. This was for two separate reasons, one being that the elders were very conscious that fights within the Pakistani community were damaging to the solidarity of their community, putting the community in a bad light in the eyes of mainstream society. The other was that the elders deplored fights between Muslims because it offended Allah. However, as mentioned earlier, there was a sense of solidarity among The Boys that served as a form of protection and, in a way, insurance. There was a form of reciprocity here, with The Boys covering each other's backs. It was the case (as we saw with Salman) that if any of The Boys was involved in a confrontation then rarely were they prepared to back down. Backing down demonstrated weakness and gave others in the neighbourhood the impression that they were scared, an image which The Boys clearly did not ever want. In his 2005 study, 'Gangstas, thugs, and hustlas', Kubrin found that if a person was assaulted it was essential in the eyes of his peers and others for him to seek revenge, otherwise he risked being victimised. There is considerable documented research which shows that the streets can also bring about violence because of the need to acquire respect by developing a reputation for being violent, by creating a self-image based on 'juice' (Anderson, 1999). Similarly, The Boys were intent on getting revenge, and, if challenged, were reluctant to give in. There was an occasion during the study when Ahmed was being threatened by another dealer. The feud had started over a drugs payment, and, although Ahmed knew this particular individual well and was aware that he was physically stronger than him, he was nevertheless not prepared to back down, as he explained after receiving constant phone calls from him:

> *Ahmed*: "He's like I owe him twelve hundred pound for *maal* [drugs] that we took off him but he was adding more and more on it. It only started at a few hundred and then next minute he's put seven, eight hundred on. He was like I'm gonna get you if you don't pay it. I said to him 'Look if you're gonna hit me then hit me, I'm not scared of you. I'll fight you if you want'. I know he'll get the better of me and that but fuck that, I'm not having him try bully me."

Ahmed was well aware that any indication of fear on his part would simply encourage others to try and push him around and take advantage, and, although he felt this situation was in a way hopeless, he was obliged to stand his ground. The Boys were conscious that if they were perceived to be weak, they were likely to find their lives rendered unbearable through bullying and harassment, perhaps encouraging those who already disliked them to persecute them. Some of The Boys had, in the past, fought with other youths from the neighbourhood, and hostilities was still very much alive, so any sign of weakness in disputes might entice others to want to seek revenge or hurt them. Meanwhile, sometimes violence could occur because other dealers from the neighbourhood were selling drugs to their customers and this was partly because of the considerable competition in the drugs market, as discussed earlier.

Conclusion

What this chapter has demonstrated is that the issue of drugs is far more complex than might be supposed. The parent generation have conflicting views on drugs and feel hopeless in the battle to motivate their young to refrain from them. The youth, like The Boys, however, often feel propelled into aspiring to become drug dealers, aware of the benefits the status of an established dealer can bring them. What's more, the variety of substances is in itself highly diverse. The skills needed to deal are highly sophisticated, despite the stigma of dealing itself. The need to find the drugs, to control quality, to find trustworthy runners, to ensure the profit margins are guaranteed, then also to be alert, not just to deceit from suppliers, runners and customers, but also entrapment and prosecution. As highlighted in this chapter, if these skills were used in the retail of any other product then they would be lauded as benefiting the economy, and that would appear to be the key to this issue. The Boys had very highly developed entrepreneurial skills, but the direction they had taken was because of a number of reasons. They struggle to obtain work, so there are no legitimate avenues to prosperity. Deprivation is a key factor in the creation of this black economy, with The Boys trapped in a situation from which they see no escape. Lack of professional qualifications and the inward-looking sense of obligation to the community restrict The Boys to the neighbourhood. Religious, family, cultural and traditional obligations mean The Boys cannot realistically contemplate life outside the area. Though stigmatised and regarded as outcasts by mainstream society, The Boys demonstrated many outstanding qualities: not just entrepreneurial skills but intense, if fractious, loyalty, a strong sense of duty to family, and a strong, if eclectic, moral code. In many ways The Boys are admirable though their good qualities are rarely visible to themselves and even less often visible to the outside world.

FIVE

Prison talk – The Boys and their experiences of 'inside'

A theme that emerged strongly from observation and conversation with The Boys was their close relationship with prison. This chapter consequently discusses this relationship, including consideration of their own experience of prison and its impact on them and their lives. An attempt is also made to assess the extent to which prison has had a beneficial or deleterious effect on the lives of The Boys. A striking aspect of prison life was how The Boys would become more devoted to Islamic faith while 'inside', and on their release would talk about Islam at some length. This chapter examines why this was the case, and what factors, if any, contributed to them becoming more religious when they were in prison. On release from prison, adjusting to outside life was at times exceptionally difficult, and the challenges faced on their release are also examined in this chapter.

We have been inside

The neighbourhood in which The Boys lived was one of ubiquitous criminalisation: everyone knew someone who was locked up [in prison]. Getting arrested, having a criminal record and going to prison were considered by The Boys as part and parcel of growing up in their neighbourhood. This also highlights the argument that youth living in deprived neighbourhoods are much more likely to offend (Sampson, 2010). Many of The Boys had themselves served custodial sentences: Kamran, Salman, Ahmed, Nav and Bash had been inside on a number of occasions. For some of The Boys prison sentences went back to a time when they were considerably younger, while for others these were much more recent. A number of The Boys had even been inside during the course of the study, as was the case for Ahmed, who went to prison for driving offences, Kamran, who was remanded for violence, and Zahir, who went to prison for drug offences.

Due to their experiences of inside, a great deal of conversation while hanging out revolved around prison, with The Boys discussing who was inside, where they were, with whom, who was released, what they were doing and reminiscing about their own experiences of being inside. One evening as we were parked up in the car, Salman and Nav were exchanging what The Boys referred to as banter when Salman recollected a time when they were in the same prison at the same time and he saw Nav become scared of a prison officer:

Salman: "It was funny as fuck. You should've seen his [Nav's] face, he was shit scared. Then he comes back in the pad [cell] and tells me that the screw [prison officer] was shouting at someone else. I was, like, shut the fuck up, I saw you through the hole. I seen your face, it was like a fucking mouse."

Nav: "Did I fuck's like, stop making up shit. I told the screw to do one and don't talk to me like that."

Salman: "Yeah, yeah, whatever. I seen you, bro, it was right outside the pad. I could hear everything, man."

The Boys, on the whole, seemed to enjoy talking about their individual experiences of prison as it seemed that memories of time spent inside gave them something to talk about when socialising. Through conversation among The Boys, one particular aspect of the prison experience that emerged was them not showing in any way that prison had been difficult. For this reason it was uncommon for them to serve their stretch [prison sentence] and on release tell the others that they had found prison difficult.

Prison was far from difficult

There was a particular image that The Boys perceived as being necessary for credibility among their peers, and this was to show that they had handled prison with ease, conscious that to openly admit that any one of them struggled to cope when inside would prove to be incredibly damaging for their credibility. Any sign of emotional expression was regarded as a sign of weakness, and therefore comments such as, "Man's gotta do his time" and "Prisons were made for people like us" were heard coming from The Boys every so often. Prison, as illustrated in several other studies, was, for The Boys, a test of their masculinity, their toughness and their street cred (Sim, 1994; Jewkes, 2002). Bash's last stretch was a few years before the study, and he, like so many of the other boys, would talk of prison as having been 'a piece of cake', recollecting how he had the best pad [cell] on the wing and how it was always full of toiletries. It is documented that, for an inmate, having a large number of toiletries is in part a display of wealth and power (Crewe, 2009).

This sense of machismo in regard to not having found prison difficult was of great importance to The Boys. Previous research has noted how there exists fierce competition for status among inmates which in itself intensifies the construction and reconstruction of male identity (Karpa, 2010). In the case of The Boys this identity was considered necessary not only within prison but, equally importantly, on their release from prison. As highlighted here, if an individual was to admit to finding prison difficult then he would be made a mockery of by the rest of The Boys and even by other youths living in the neighbourhood. This was to become apparent one evening when hanging around on the streets and some of The Kids noticed Ahmed driving past. On seeing The Kids, Ahmed stopped the car and greeted them, asking them how they were doing. Majid then asked Ahmed how he had handled prison, as Ahmed had been released only a few days previously, making a point of mentioning how he had heard from Zahir that Ahmed had found prison difficult. Ahmed, who was conscious that his reputation would be damaged if he openly admitted this, replied furiously: "He's [Zahir] a little shit. Tell him to say it to my face. I admit that I was a bit down and that. What does he know? I had a lot going on outside, not like him, but I wasn't stressing like he's making out. He's full of shit."

What emerged from Ahmed's response was the importance of being seen to be able to handle the experience of imprisonment with aplomb. Any implication that they were not would have huge ramifications for The Boys. If it was the case that one of them found the experience difficult, then rarely would he openly admit that in front of the others, as was the case with Ahmed. However, several days later when I was with Ahmed in his car, he opened up, sharing his experiences of being inside: "Armley [prison] was fucking shit, it was so depressing man. The screws don't give a fuck 'bout you, they don't care. The food was shit and the bang-up [time spent in the cell] got to me – it was too much for me."

It was surprising, in many ways, to hear what Ahmed was saying as he never gave the impression in front of the others that he had found prison difficult. He had also spent a significantly longer period in prison a few years prior to this stretch, so it was bewildering to know why he found it difficult on this particular occasion. This leads to the perhaps surprising inference that familiarity with prison does not always mean The Boys will handle it well, but instead there can be fluctuations between resilience, endurance and psychological damage inflicted by the experience. It can depend on what prison The Boys were in, how they were treated by fellow inmates and prison officers, and how much support they had from family and friends while inside.

In Ahmed's case, there were several factors that contributed to him finding prison difficult. To begin with, he was in a prison with which he was not familiar. His previous sentences had been in a different prison, one which he felt had better facilities for inmates. Another factor was that he was in a relationship, and he was fearful that any time spent away from his girlfriend could potentially damage this relationship (this later proved to be the case – after his release Ahmed was no longer with this particular girl, who was now in a relationship with someone whom he knew and whom he now held a vendetta against).

Prison bought back bad memories

Incarceration often came at considerable personal cost for some of The Boys, bringing back bad memories such as the loss of a family member or of a close friend. Research has highlighted how young people involved in offending experience parental, multiple and traumatic deaths at a higher frequency than in the general population (Vaswani, 2008). Nav experienced bereavement while he was in prison, but, unlike the other Boys who had lost friends and extended family members, it was Nav's father who had unexpectedly passed away. The death of his father was something that Nav found extremely upsetting, and he would occasionally, while hanging out, talk about it to The Boys. One evening as we were sitting in the car, Nav unexpectedly became emotional speaking of how he felt when he first learned about his father's death when he was in prison:

> *Nav*: "I couldn't believe it, I was in shock, I jus' wanted to be there for my mum and brothers but I couldn't. Them days were tough for me, I felt like I could kill someone that's how angry I used to be. All I used to think about was my dad and how hard he worked to make life easy for us. I was, like, proper down for ages."

Nav was allowed to attend his father's funeral prayer and, while he was grateful he could attend, this left him feeling embarrassed for his family as he was accompanied into the mosque by two prison officers:

> *Nav*: "Me cousins, especially my uncles – I know they didn't like me, they were there in the *masjid*– [place of worship], they were, like, looking at me. I knew what they

were thinking, they were, like, he's not there for his family when they need him. But then I didn't say anything because there were loads of people in there, it was rammed. It was hard. I felt that I had stressed my dad out because of getting locked up and that."

Often major family events would occur from which The Boys were excluded, and no compassionate discretion was given to allow prisoners to attend the funerals of close relatives without the presence of prison guards. This was especially important to The Boys when the funeral was that of a parent and was held in the mosque in view of all those present. There was also a feeling, as Nav mentions, of him having let the family down for not being there when they were going through such a difficult time. This is a particularly interesting point because, despite The Boys not being prepared to show anyone that prison was testing at times, they would speak of prison as not allowing them to be able to support their families during tough times.

It's hard to keep out of trouble when inside

Through conversation with The Boys it became apparent that while in prison, they felt it was difficult to keep away from trouble and we discuss why this was the case in this section. One reason was that there was a need to stand up for themselves. They were concerned not to be seen as weak by other inmates, aware that if this was ever the case then they risked being intimidated by them. Research has highlighted how exchanges with inmates often serve as tests of nerve and character (Toch, 1992), with inmates being aware of other inmates monitoring their behaviour so as to judge how able or willing they are to defend themselves (Wortley, 2002). One evening as we were sitting in his flat, Bash started telling The Boys in some detail about a fight which he had with an inmate who was trying to intimidate him on his arrival in prison:

> Bash: "I went in there [prison] and man was new so I didn't really know what's what. It was like just get on with yer own business. I didn't care about anything else cuz I was on some heavy charges. Well anyway, I'm on association and this *kala* [black guy], I mean a proper big lad, I swear proper hench [big], he was like twice the size of Jameel, he comes to me and says, 'I want your canteen' [belongings]. At first I was, like, what the fuck, then he says to me that

'This is my wing and I got it on lockdown'. I knew what
the fucker was up to, so I said to him, 'Come to my pad.' I
had some tuna tins in a sock and I just blasted him all over
the place, the fucker was clean out. The screws [prison
officers] found out and put me down block [segregation],
but I was lucky that nothing happened to me or aught.I
came back to the wing the next day."

As Bash illustrates, The Boys felt it was necessary to stand up for
themselves when inside otherwise they risked being targeted by fellow
inmates. This was also highlighted on a separate occasion when one
Friday afternoon, after attending *Jumma* [Friday prayers] with Shaf and
Ali, we bumped into Zahir (one of The Kids). I had met Zahir a while
back, in fact it was in the first year of the study when The Boys stopped
to talk to him near Zaks, and when he had told them that he was up
for sentencing in the Crown Court the next day. Anyway, time had
gone by, with Zahir having served his stretch, and now released from
prison early on tag [with an electronic device on his ankle]. The Boys,
as well as a number of local youths, had gathered outside the mosque
to meet with Zahir, all intrigued to know how he had found prison.
Zahir appeared well and confident, telling The Boys that he handled
prison with ease. He then spoke of how there were some inmates
inside who would try and intimidate others by outright bullying and
by taking their belongings from them and that there were others who
would exaggerate and blatantly lie about their convictions:

> *Zahir:* "There was this guy who I was padded up [shared a
> cell] with and he was, like, I'm sleeping on the top bunk,
> I was, like, are you fuck, he was giving the big one but I
> soon put him in his place. It was bullshit inside though.
> You meet some right people, they just chat right shit. They
> were, like, making out that they were on top and that [had
> a street credibility on the outside], and that they got done
> for big things, but I weren't stupid. I knew that most were
> just nobodies, jus' trying to blag my head. Come on, people
> who are in for big things don't need to open their mouth
> and chat shit. They stay quiet and don't let anyone know
> anything."

Street credibility was hugely significant to The Boys, an inverse form
of status. As highlighted previously, the urge for status would lead
some of The Boys to boast that they had been convicted of more

serious crimes than they had in fact committed. One reason for this was, as research has highlighted, they were aware that the more serious the crime they committed then the higher the status for them. It is reported that crimes such as murder or robbing a bank occupy the apex of the hierarchy of kudos, with petty crimes and sexual offences at its base (Vaughn and Sapp, 1989; Winfree et al, 2002; Jewkes, 2005). Consequently, it is also well documented that inmates who commit crimes such as rape and paedophilia risk being targeted for extreme levels of physical and psychological victimisation by fellow inmates (Spencer, 2009). To avoid such a mark of disgust, it has been noted that sex offenders will try and pass as non-sex offenders (Tan and Grace, 2008) by telling inmates that they had committed other crimes. However, in some instances hiding the crime that one committed from fellow inmates can be exceptionally difficult for the inmate. This was illustrated when Bash spoke one day of what had happened to a fellow Pakistani prisoner when he and other inmates on the wing found out that he was not in for drugs offences as he had told them but was, in fact, convicted of rape:

> Bash: "There was this *apna* [Pakistani] guy from down south, and there's this one time we were all on association, and *banda* [people] were, like, he can't be in for drugs. He ain't got a clue, I mean he's proper *saada* [simple], but then there was this guy who was in the same prison as him before, and he moved onto our wing, and he tells us that he's a nonce [rapist], so we all pounced on him [attacked him]. They had to move him onto protection."

Often commentators, including those in positions of power and authority, watch the young men who get into trouble and comment with a degree of glibness on their own responsibility for what happens to them. While at one level this is true, at the same time, with regard to The Boys, such commentary frequently shows a serious lack of insight into the subtle, hidden factors which often propel them into trouble, even at times against their own will. The idea of defending themselves – defending their religion, family, friends and being seen as honourable – can be major issues which are factors in types of behaviour leading to trouble. The importance of machismo, of not losing face in front of fellow inmates is very important. These behaviours are often motivated by very high standards and ideals, and what happens in prison can even at times affect their status on the outside. Butler (2008) and others have similarly highlighted how prisoners may have friends or associates detained in prison, and how they behave in prison can impact on their identity in the community. The Boys were well aware of this and were conscious of never wanting to lose face whether it be inside or in their neighbourhood.

Stand by fellow Pakistani inmates

The Boys, as discussed earlier, spoke of demonstrating solidarity to one another and also to fellow Pakistani inmates who were in the same prison as them. Wilson's (2003) study in a young offenders institution described how young black men would demonstrate support and solace to other black prisoners. In the same way, Pakistani prisoners, through their shared ethnicity and religion, combined to demonstrate solidarity in what can be termed a hostile environment. This sense of solidarity helped The Boys to look out for, protect and defend each other and other Pakistani inmates. This was illustrated when Ali spoke of a fight that took place when he was in prison and how he and other Pakistani inmates felt obliged to demonstrate solidarity to a fellow Pakistani prisoner who had been attacked by white inmates:

> *Ali*: "These *goras* [white inmates] rushed [attacked] an *apna* [Pakistani inmate] in the showers, they smashed him up big time, should have seen his face, looked proper bad. Anyway, the next day on exercise we seen the *gora* and fucked one of them up, the screws [prison officers] had to put the full wing on lockdown because of it."

Another example of The Boys demonstrating solidarity to fellow Pakistani inmates was highlighted when we were stood in the takeaway one evening eagerly waiting the food we had ordered. Salman told the others how he would 'look out' for the guy who was now working in the takeaway when they were inside together:

> *Salman*: "I took care of him. He was getting bullied by some *goras* [white lads] from Barnsley sides, they used to get him to clean their pads [cells]. Felt sorry for him, so I told them to leave him alone and told him to chill [spend time] with us on exercise. If it weren't for me they would have just carried on bullying the poor bastard."

If one had shown solidarity to fellow Pakistani inmates then one would expect this to be appreciated and recognised. When Salman was not given any discount on his food order from the person working at the takeaway, this left him feeling rather annoyed! "I should have let the *goras* [white inmates] fuck him up, can't believe he didn't give me a discount, if anything he should have given me it on the house, especially what I did for him."

It seemed that there was an expectation from fellow Pakistani inmates whom they knew that they would stick together, and this was something that Ahmed spoke on his release from prison as being a difficult choice:

> *Ahmed*: "You go in there, and the boys you see in there ask you if you're down with them [allies]. You, like, know in your head that if you're down with them and they get in a fight then you'll end up down block [segregated] and even an outside charge [a new criminal charge]. But then the thing is if you get in a fight then you need them to be down with you so it's hard, to be honest."

As Ahmed highlights, 'being down' for fellow Pakistani inmates could result in violence and potentially an outside charge, and this was something that he was astute enough to establish, but then realised that if he expected the support of others then he had to show them solidarity. However, while solidarity with fellow Pakistani prisoners was an important aspect of life for The Boys in prison, there were some among them who felt that this was no longer comparable to the solidarity of the past. According to Bash, the first time he ever went inside Pakistani boys from Bradford would always stick together, but he felt this was no longer like it used to be, as he spoke about one evening:

> *Bash*: "When I got locked before all of us boys [Pakistanis] used to stick together and if any one of us got into a fight, then we all got stuck in, but it's not like that anymore because this time when I went inside I saw some *apnas* [Pakistanis] fighting against *apnas*. Some of the local lads were even trying to bully each other. It felt more like every man for himself in there now."

Grudges among local Pakistani boys were sometimes settled in prison. It was common to hear The Boys speak of fights that had taken place between rival groups from Bradford who were currently inside. Previous research has also documented how turf wars from the street can find their way into prison as inmates are packed together, leaving few options for retreat to a safe and neutral spot (Tewksbury, 2006). One evening as we sat in Bash's flat, The Boys were talking about prison, the conversation having started when they had heard that a particular Pakistani individual whom they knew had been badly beaten by another Pakistani inmate from Bradford. According to The Boys the feud between the two lads had existed for several years, and it was only when they both ended up on the same wing in prison that one of the lads chose to take revenge against the other.

Meanwhile, solidarity in prison also meant being generous to one another. In the third year of the study when Ahmed was released from prison, he spoke of having met Kamran inside and said how Kamran took it on himself to look after him:

> *Ahmed*: "Kamran was a top lad. When he saw me on *Jumma* [Friday prayers] he asked me if I needed anything. He told me he had a phone and if I needed it I could have it. He had *kali* [hash] on him, it was 'bout a quarter, but the thing is in there it's worth a lot more. You know I didn't smoke any of it cuz it had been plugged up man's arse, so I sold it for burn [cigarettes], cuz when I came in the canteen [weekly shopping list] had been done, and I had to wait another week till the next canteen."

One of the supreme ironies of prison was that The Boys were often incarcerated for drug dealing but then proceeded to deal drugs while in prison, sometimes outwitting the guards in order to do so. Research has documented increasing concern with the way in which some Muslim inmates are able to get involved in drugs while they are in prison (Crewe, 2009). A number of The Boys spoke of having sold drugs when they were inside, saying that drugs were worth considerably more in the prison environment. While sitting in Shah's girlfriend's flat one evening, Ahmed and Ali were discussing how they would smuggle and sell drugs when they were inside before considering sending some drugs to a friend who was still in prison:

Ali: "I used to get as much as I wanted, I mean loads of it [spice], I had mans [friends] bringing it on visits for someone [another inmate] and I'd get it from them on the wing. People were proper dying for it, they'd be off their heads all fucking day from it."

Ahmed: "I'm thinking of sending some *chesa* [drugs] in for Khan, he phoned me the other day and was, like,

> drop some off to this girl's house for him so she'd
> take it in for him on a visit."

Drug dealing in prison may seem a complete nonsense to the outsider unfamiliar with life in jail. However, as The Boys mentioned, it was second nature to find ways round the system to earn money and to deaden the boredom and anaesthetise the misery of life inside. Another way in which to ease the boredom while inside was for The Boys to turn to the Islamic faith, and this impacted significantly on the lives of The Boys when they were inside, as discussed below.

Prison helped increase *Emaan*

A prominent theme that emerged from The Boys' accounts of prison was how many of them would become much more devoted to Islamic faith [*Emaan*] while they there. Islam has a particular appeal among inmates, and this is confirmed by the seemingly high rates of conversion in prison (Waller, 2003; Ammar et al, 2004; Hamm, 2009). While there has been some research exploring why inmates convert to Islam when inside (Spalek and El-Hassan, 2007), relatively little remains to be known about why Muslim prisoners become more devoted to religion when they are imprisoned. The aim of this section is to understand what factors (if any) caused or motivated The Boys to become more devoted to Islamic faith when they were inside.

Those of The Boys who went to prison during the course of the study appeared, on their release, to have become much more devoted to Islam. Ahmed was praying regularly at the mosque on his release, and would even speak to the others at times about how he now wanted to become a better Muslim. Similarly, Zahir appeared more devoted when released from prison, having grown a small beard and outwardly showing this commitment by wearing his prayer beads around his neck. Nav, who these days rarely prayed even the *Jumma* [Friday prayers], spoke of never having missed any prayers when he was inside, and there were similar accounts from the others who had been in prison. According to The Boys, fellow Pakistani inmates also appeared to demonstrate more devotion to Islamic faith when they were inside. This was highlighted when we were hanging out in the car one day and Shaf asked Zahir how a particular individual who lived in the neighbourhood and who several months earlier had received a lengthy prison sentence for drugs offences was doing:

Shaf: "How was Teja doing? Poor bastard got slammed
               [received a long sentence]. Eh, but got to say he
               was living the high life before he went in, I seen
               him rolling [driving] in a 50-grand car week before
               he got locked up."
Zahir: "I know, it's his own fault, he bought it on top for
               himself, he was all right in there [in prison], he
               seemed a bit stressed at first but he was cool after a
               bit. He's gone proper into the *Deen* [Islamic way].
               He was always praying and that and on association
               [free time] he'd be speaking about *Deen* and giving
               Dawah [preaching about Islam]."

Going into prison can be difficult, especially for the first time and for
those who enjoyed a lavish lifestyle. The shock of being stripped of
all the accoutrements of their wealth – their cars, clothes and suchlike
– added to this stress. Religion, it seemed, offered them a feeling
of purpose and comfort. It could be argued that faith was a coping
strategy in difficult times (Liebling and Maruna, 2005). Research has
also highlighted how inmates find turning to religion a coping strategy
(Koenig, 1995; Maruna, Wilson and Curran, 2006). One evening as
we were cruising in the car Salman spoke of how, on his last stretch,
he would pray the five daily prayers and how, by doing so, this helped
him to relax in his cell:

> *Salman*: "I used to pray loads when I was inside. I used to
> have a proper good routine, I'd read Quran every day. I
> remember I used to even wake up for *Fajr* [sunrise prayer],
> I used to tell the night screws [prison officers] to wake me
> up. If I missed my *Salah* [prayer] I'd be all stressed, but then
> when I prayed it was like a buzz for me. But then when I
> got out it all changed. I mean, I did, like, read Quran and
> that for a while, but then slowly things changed, I started
> chilling again. I forgot 'bout my *Deen* [religion]."

The newly found devotion that The Boys would find inside did not
tend to last long after release from prison. A number of them spoke of
slowly seeing this devotion fade, and they no longer prayed as often as
they did. Research has also documented this phenomenon (Maruna
et al, 2006). However, another reason why The Boys would become
more religious when they were inside was that they had a lot more
time on their hands. Praying gave them something to do: as Salman has

already mentioned, Islam offered him a routine. Praying the five daily prayers that Muslims are obliged to pray helped in keeping The Boys active while in their cells with little else to do other than watch TV.

> *Kamran*: "There used to be fuck all to do. I was sick to death of watching fucking Jeremy Kyle and all the other bullshit that used to come on TV, so I thought fuck this, I may as well start praying my *namaza* [five daily prayers] and do something good at least."

It seemed that religion gave The Boys structure to their day and a level of dignity not possible to achieve at the hands of cellmates or prison officers. Free from worldly distractions, it facilitated adherence to the outward observances required.

A further possible explanation for The Boys showing more devotion to faith while they were inside was to do with reflection. It is well documented that being imprisoned can cause individuals to see the web of meaning that they may have previously taken for granted (Cohen and Taylor, 1972). This realisation can lead inmates to reflect on issues such as their existence, life and death and other issues which are often bracketed out when on the outside. The Boys would speak about inside as helping them to feel that they were making the most of a difficult situation through considerable reflection in what could be termed seclusion. This was something that even the Imam at the local mosque spoke about one Friday, telling worshippers that seclusion helped Muslims increase their devoutness. The Imam was principally referring to a religious practice, wherein the last ten days of Ramadan are considered better and more righteous for Muslims to spend in seclusion. In trying to highlight the benefit of *Itikaaf* [spending the last ten days of Ramadan in seclusion], the Imam gave the example of people who were in prison:

> "I see brothers coming out of prison coming to the mosques. Then what happens to them is that the *Duniya* [the world] hits them. They see boys in fast cars, see women dressed in short skirts and what do they do, they begin to chase the *Duniya*. They slowly stop coming to the mosque, and what happens is that they lose their *Emaan* [faith]. They stop praying altogether and they go back to how they used to be before they went into prison. The question is why they prayed in prison: they prayed in prison because they

were locked up for 23 hours a day, they didn't have the distractions that we have out here."

Another explanation for The Boys showing increased devotion to their Islamic faith when inside was a realisation that their lives were lives in which they were doing considerable wrong. There were some among The Boys who, like Ali, spoke of turning to Allah [God] for forgiveness. Previous literature has found that turning to God for forgiveness is a key explanation why prisoners turn to religion, in the hope that they can be forgiven for their past crimes (Maruna et al, 2006). In the same way as Islam, Christianity has the potential to offer inmates a path to what can be termed a new life, one in which the past is considered to be wiped clean when turning to God. Ali: "I knew if I repented for what I did, Allah would forgive me, I knew it's not, like, I killed someone. Look, everyone deserves a second chance, nobody's perfect and Allah says in the Quran turn to me and ask me to forgive you and I will forgive you."

Being imprisoned consequently gave many of The Boys a sense that they were in many ways better Muslims when inside than outside. They felt that they were refraining from many of the sins that they were involved in on the outside. Although drugs were readily available inside, and some of The Boys were involved with them, other temptations such as drinking alcohol or womanising could not be indulged in, so, by praying, many of The Boys felt that they were better Muslims. This was to become apparent when one evening The Boys were conversing over prison when Ahmed spoke of refraining from sin when he was inside:

> *Ahmed*: "When you're inside you can't do the *Guna* [sins] that you did before. I know I used to have a smoke [cannabis] inside but that's all really, I wasn't doing anything else bad, like I do now. I wasn't sleeping with gals, I wasn't drinking, if anything I was praying more."

With The Boys turning more religious when they were inside, a concern was that incarceration was counterproductive because while in prison young Muslim men are much more likely to be exposed to radicalisation, not merely because of the stigma of a prison sentence that excluded The Boys from mainstream society, effectively pushing them back into reoffending. A recent report titled *Roots of Violent Radicalisation* identified prisons as one of the major breeding grounds for terrorists recruiting young Muslims into extremism (House of Commons Home Affairs Committee, 2015). It is also reported that young Muslim men who offend are at much greater risk of becoming radicalised than those who do not offend. Take for example, Muktar Said Ibrahim, the leader in the failed 'second wave' attack on the London transport system in 2005, who had previously served time in a juvenile institution, with some reports suggesting that it was while he was in prison that he became radicalised (Hamm, 2009). Consequently, there was a danger that The Boys were at greater risk of becoming radicalised on entering prison, but, from the time spent with The Boys, it did not appear that they were in anyway radicalised in their views on Islam, although there were some who did speak of trying to implement Islamic values in their homes on release.

> *Kamran*: "Before I went in [prison] I didn't say anything to my sister for not wearing the hijab [headscarf worn by Muslim women], but then when I got out I told her she had to start wearing hijab. I told her it's a big sin for Muslim women to not wear hijab, and she listened."

Meanwhile, some of The Boys spoke of having met some Muslim inmates who they felt were radicalised in their interpretations of Islamic faith when they were inside, some of whom would even preach their views openly to other inmates:

> *Salman*: "There were these two Muslims, one was a new Muslim [convert], on the wing, and they were always going around telling peeps [Muslim inmates] to pray and that and to give up our TVs, and if they seen us chilling with non-Muslims, they'd say stop talking with them, they're dirty people."

While one could argue that, because of their age, The Boys were less likely to be easily influenced by radicals when inside, there was, however, a danger that some of The Kids who at present showed little interest or devotion to Islamic faith ran a far greater risk of becoming radicalised when they went inside. The reason for this, as discussed in Chapters Four and Six, was that The Kids were much more naive and gullible in comparison with The Boys.

Prison was hostile territory for Muslims

The Boys' experiences of the inside were often of hostility and racism. Many of The Boys spoke of having experienced racism, much of which came from other inmates but some of which also came from prison officers. It is well documented that ethnic minority prisoners complain of racial incidents significantly more than whites (Bhui, 2009; Case et al., 2017). *Muslim Prisoners' Experiences: A Thematic Review* (Bhui, 2010) found that, overall, 46% of Muslim prisoners felt unsafe compared with 36% of non-Muslim prisoners. According to The Boys, there were some prison officers who were blatantly racist towards them and whom they felt did not like them because they were Muslims. This, they felt, was evident from the way in which they were treated.

There was a strong sense of feeling among The Boys that, because Muslims are often depicted in the media as terrorists and responsible for gruesome crimes, hatred of Muslims within UK prisons has sharply increased. One evening Nav spoke of how, when he went into a certain prison which he referred to as 'up north', fellow white inmates would repeatedly shout racist abuse out of their windows at him and other Muslim inmates:

> *Nav*: "The *goras* [white inmates] be, like, saying there's another Muslim rapist on our wing and saying we were all groomers and terrorists and that. They'd then be shouting out how Muslims are going to get it [get hurt], but the screws [prison officers] did fuck all. They could hear it but they didn't give a shit to be honest."

The Boys felt that prison officers, as highlighted by Nav's comments, would turn a blind eye to racism aimed at them and fellow Muslim prisoners by white racist inmates. This is something that has previously been evidenced in the death of a 19-year-old Muslim inmate, Zahid Mubarek, who was murdered by his cellmate Robert Stewart. Stewart was known by the prison authorities to be a violent racist with mental health problems (Bowling and Phillips, 2002), but it is reported that, despite this, they had turned a blind eye (*The Guardian*, 5 October 2001). Similarly, Genders and Player's 1989 study, a decade before Mubarek was killed, uncovered that prison officers would place black and racist white inmates in the same cells to stir up trouble. The Boys, as previously mentioned, felt that prison officers did not like them because they were Muslims. Bhui (2009: 90) highlights that 'Forty per cent of Muslims, compared to 22% of non-Muslims, said they had been victimized by staff'. It is well documented that Muslim inmates are more likely than their Christian counterparts to be treated unfairly in practising their religion – for example, with regard to special dietary needs, place and times of worship, and suitable ministers (see Burnett and Farrell, 1994: 21–3; also Horabin, 1978; Ahmed, 2001; Weller et al, 2001: 53; Spalek and Wilson, 2002). One day as we were cruising in the car Ahmed and Salman were discussing their time inside when Salman started talking about a particular prison officer who he recalled as disliking Muslims:

Salman: "He [prison officer] was always trying to be a funny fucker. He'd open our door the last on visits even when it was *Jumma* [Friday prayers], it'd be like him trying to make us go late."

Jameel: "You could see it in their [prison officers] faces that they didn't like Muslims. It was like they were doing their job but at the same time holding back hatred for us."

Similarly, some of The Boys spoke of how they were treated differently from white inmates when in prison. Ahmed described how all the good jobs would be given to white prisoners and Muslims would have "the shitty jobs". In the same way, Genders and Player's (1989) study *Race Relations in Prisons*, commissioned by the Home Office, found that ethnic minority inmates were significantly less likely to be employed in the best jobs compared with white inmates. As for Nav, he felt that he was not given his 'Cat D' [allowed to go to an open, Category D, prison], while several white inmates who, from his perspective had criminal records which were much worse than his, had been moved to open prison. Nav felt that this showed double standards by the prison authorities, and he blamed it on racism. Another factor fuelling resentment and negative perceptions by The Boys of mainstream society and the judicial system was that, once they were imprisoned, they found non-Muslim prisoners who had committed equivalent if not more serious crimes, but who had received lighter sentences than they had. The only apparent difference, according to The Boys, was their ethnicity and religious affiliation.

Adjusting to the 'outside world' was difficult

Release from prison is often difficult, as adjusting to the outside world can be demanding for inmates (Pager, 2003). Lost time cannot be recaptured (Jamieson and Grounds, 2005), and this has also been documented by prisoner autobiographies (Cook and Wilkinson, 1998). The Boys found release from prison to be challenging, and some of them spoke of the difficulties they experienced adapting to the change in environments. Anecdotally, this is well illustrated by the story of Salman who, at the conclusion of his sentence, spoke of how the following morning he was unable to leave his bedroom until a family member came and allowed him out. Although this sounds comical, in reality it indicates that The Boys, as well as so many ex-prisoners, had great difficulty adjusting back to the outside world. Time spent in jail is time of de-individualisation and the institutionalisation of the personality. The longer the sentence and the more frequent the imprisonments, the greater the difficulties some of The Boys had in adjusting to civilian life. At the same time, there is a tacit recognition between them that they all need support, ranging from money to moral support, at this time. While the purpose of prison is to deprive an offender of his liberty as a punishment, the reality is that prison carries with it many damaging, long-term hidden costs, many of which are psychological and emotional (Bukstel and Kilmann, 1980).

Prison also impacted on the breakdown of family relationships as, on release from prison, some of The Boys found it difficult to get on with their family members, particularly after having served a long stretch. This was the case with Kamran who, when out of prison, was not getting on well with his siblings, whom he felt were not showing him the respect that he deserved as an older brother, and this, as he explained one day to the others, was the cause of most of the arguments that he was having with his parents:

> *Kamran*: "They [parents] always taking me younger brother's side. I know why though, its cuz he gives them money and I don't. He's a fucking prick though, he thinks he's all clever getting brave in front of them, but you should see him when he's on his own, he don't say two words. But then in front of them, he starts getting all funny. I told him the other day to pass me the remote, asked him about ten times and he ignored me so I just lamped him [punched him]."

In fact, I had noticed from the time that I had spent with Kamran (before he again returned to prison) that he struggled with the adjustment to the outside world. According to the others, this was because he was familiar with prison and he found it difficult to cope with the pressures on the outside. Nav said, "Kamran prefers prison. He doesn't like it on the out, he feels lost and that out here." Although it was clear over the course of the study that Kamran did not deliberately go looking to get back inside, his actions were, nevertheless, careless and dangerous at times. He had, in total, spent seven years of his life in prison, and one could argue that he was in many ways familiar with a life that he was so conditioned to. Maintaining relationships with family and friends with shrewdness was something that he found to be difficult. Kamran, as discussed in Chapter Four, was blunt, and his bluntness caused him to be in arguments and disagreements with others which could at times lead him to become involved in violence.

It is important to highlight here that it seemed, in the case of The Boys, that prison did not reduce offending. If anything, it was seen by them as a hindrance to their offending, and they would come out only to continue to do what they were doing before they went inside. Some of The Boys were eager to make more money on release from prison, keen to catch up on the time they had lost inside. Zahir, on his release, returned to selling drugs:

> *Zahir.* "There's not a lot for me to do now that I'm out. I'm trying not to get back into hustling [drug dealing] but it's harder now. What else can I do to make paper [money]? I have made a few good links in there [prison] and I can get my hands on bagging shit now, so I will wait and see what I do. In the meantime I'm just gonna chill and enjoy myself."

Time spent inside did, however, make it difficult for some of The Boys to get back into the drugs market as other dealers were quick to take their clientele, but contacts made inside with other inmates could, in some cases, make it more profitable in selling drugs on release. Some of The Boys spoke of making "good links inside", and were now able to buy drugs cheaper than they had previously.

Conclusion

While the relationship between The Boys and prison is complex, even a superficial analysis shows that prison has failed to help The Boys refrain from subsequent post-prison offending. This is clearly not a straightforward issue as it appears to be the same for many others who have served custodial sentences and who have gone on to reoffend. Meanwhile, what we learn from this chapter is that prison was hostile ground for many of The Boys who faced racism directed at them not only from other inmates but also from some prison officers too. However, an interesting aspect of time served inside was how many of The Boys appeared to taken a keen interest in their Islamic faith and how this would continue for a short while on release. As also mentioned in this chapter, release from prison was not easy for The

Boys who were faced by a number of challenges, and this is certainly an area requiring further research.

From The Boys' accounts of prison, what becomes obvious is that prison has not been the reason for desisting from crime, nor does the thought of going to prison scare them. If anything, prison was considered by them to be a place to become a better Muslim, or even in some cases make better contacts with drug dealers from other towns and cities who were also inside. This point was brought to the surface by Jameel, who spoke one evening of being worried when he went to prison for the first time but then realising when he got there that it was not as bad as he had anticipated, and later making a number of contacts with fellow inmates who sold drugs and from whom he was able to buy drugs on his release.

SIX

The impact of Pakistani culture and Islamic faith on the lives of The Boys

The first half of this chapter focuses on the role that Pakistani culture played in the lives of The Boys while the second explores the relationship The Boys had with their Islamic faith. The reason why it was important to explore the influence of Pakistani culture and Islam on the lives of the young men in the study was that it has been noted that Pakistanis living in the UK bear complex identities, with a strong cultural heritage and also as Muslims (Werbner, 2004). Some commentators have noted that multiple sets of values cause second- and third-generation Pakistanis to suffer an 'identity conflict' (Archer, 2001; Cressey, 2002) and for this reason these were necessary to explore.

This chapter starts by examining the relationship The Boys had with their ancestral rather than native Pakistani culture and explores some of the challenges they found with certain aspects of Pakistani culture. It then moves on to uncover The Boys' thoughts and experiences of Pakistan, a place which they would refer to frequently as 'back home', a country that all had visited during some stage of their lives. The Boys, as discussed in Chapter Five considered Islamic faith to be incredibly important to them, and this chapter explores why. It seemed odd at first glance that The Boys considered Islamic faith to be imperative because they were troublesome delinquents who drank alcohol, slept around with girls and were involved with the consumption and sale of drugs. It is precisely the tension between all these aspects of their relationship with faith that made it interesting to study The Boys' perception of Islam and what role, if any, Islam played in their lives and in their thinking.

Pakistani culture is challenging

Being born in Britain but in homes that adhere to traditional values of Pakistan can be a bewildering experience for some young Pakistani people (Anwar and Hussain, 2013). While an amazing number are able to straddle such contrasting cultures with great stability, it is clear that for some second- and third-generation Pakistanis this can be a difficult balancing act to accomplish (The Change Institute, 2009). There can be a sense of having to choose one or the other, rather than eclectically selecting from both and creating a synthesis.

According to the Pakistani parental generation, there were important reasons to cling onto Pakistani culture in the UK because British culture had, in their eyes, lost central morals such as family values, sexual restraint out of marriage, hard work and self-reliance (Bolognani, 2009). As a consequence, Pakistani parents encouraged their children growing up in the UK to learn about their traditions and speak their mother tongue (Wardak, 2000), in the hope that they would refrain from adverse behaviours. Preserving an already familiar culture has been a natural thing to do for migrants from foreign countries and the reason for this, as Wallman (1986) has noted, is that ethnicity cannot be sustained in the head alone, it needs an environment that will enable one to live one's ethnicity through action. However, many British Pakistani youth have today gradually become distant from traditional ways (Quraishi, 2005; Anwar and Hussain, 2013), adopting British culture and rebelling against the culture of their parents.

The Boys were in many ways distant from their traditional culture. They would often speak of how traditional culture was tedious and had little relevance to their lives in the UK. There were a number of cultural traditions which The Boys could not comprehend. This was the case with two particular cultural practices: Pakistani funerals and weddings.

The Boys felt that the cultural practice of *Purees*[1], maintained by the elders was frustrating. *Purees* would be held at either a house or nearby mosque with members of the community and friends paying their respects to anyone who had lost a family member. One particular aspect of this tradition which The Boys found most annoying was the fact that people would sit around for a considerable time, and often do so without making any conversation. In some cases it is known that *Purees* can last for up to four days. It was to become apparent how The Boys found sitting at *Purees* difficult as was the time they went to pray the funeral prayer of an elder in the local mosque one evening. After the prayer they felt obliged to sit at the mosque, but were unable to sit for long: Bash, clearly finding sitting on the floor uncomfortable, walked out. Later when asked by the others why he had walked out, he explained to Ali and Salman that the practice of *Purees* had taken its origin from Hinduism and had no relevance to Islamic faith:

> Bash: "I can't sit in there man, it's proper stupid just sitting there and people looking at each other without saying nothing. It's [*Purees*] not even Islamic, it's from the Hindus,

it's when our ancestors in Pakistan were Hindus, they used to do this and they've just carried on over the years. Check it out, bro, if you don't believe me."

Another example of Pakistani cultural practices that The Boys found annoying was around weddings. They would occasionally express how, in their view, Pakistani weddings were tiring and exhausting, lasting several days. This was highlighted in conversation one day between Ahmed and Salman when Ahmed had to take his parents to a family wedding:

Ahmed:	"I got to take me mum and dad to Birmingham next weekend to a wedding. It's me cousin's wedding but, you know what, I can't be fucking arsed to go there, it's gonna be a full weekend shit."
Salman:	"Why don't you get your dad to drive so you don't have to go?"
Ahmed:	"Me old man don't like to drive on the motorway and there's no one else who's going from here. *Kasmay* [honestly] I would much rather stay here chilling with you lot then going all that way to spend time with cousins who I don't fucking like anyway."

However, despite The Boys finding certain cultural practices boring they nevertheless felt a need to show sensibility to the sensitivities of elders by outwardly abiding by Pakistani cultural practices, as highlighted by Ahmed above. But having said this, The Boys would secretly adjust to the sensibilities of the dominant culture, and there were two key areas which bought this to the forefront more than others. One was the growth in consumption of alcohol among The Boys, and the other was their relationships with girls, as we discuss next.

Relationships with girls was a contentious issue

Traditional Pakistani culture means that, in most cases, parents will arrange marriages for their children (Qureshi et al, 2014), with Pakistani parents encouraging their children to marry individuals of the same ethnicity and religion as themselves (Shaw, 2000). Research has noted how marrying within one's ethnic group maintains the ethno-religious identity of the group by keeping its cultural purity (Modood et al, 1994; Basit, 1997a; Shaw, 2000). However, since many of The Boys did not feel ready to get married and were unable to have relationships with local Pakistani girls unless they were married to them, this drove many of the lads to seek sexual fulfilment with non-Pakistani girls, in particular with white British girls who lived in other areas of Bradford.

It became clear through observation that The Boys were popular with white British girls. There were occasions during the study when some of them were hounded with phone calls and messages from girls who they knew. Bash and Kamran's phone would almost always be ringing when hanging out, receiving phone calls and text messages. There were times during the study when some of The Boys would read aloud messages that they had received from girls they knew. One day when we were at the local snooker hall, Bash, who was sitting watching The Boys play snooker, was texting a certain girl and would every so often call Salman over to show him messages he had just received: "Check this one out, she wants to meet up with me tonight, she's asking me to take her to a posh restaurant first but fuck that, I ain't spending that much time with her, I'd rather just take her to hotel and smash her" [have sex with her].

On another evening as we were cruising around in the car, Kamran's phone kept ringing and he was ignoring whoever it was that was calling him, so Ali asked him about it.

Ali:	"Who's that calling you, bro?"
Kamran:	"It's that gal [girl] from the other day, the one I met outside KFC. I knew I shouldn't have given her my number, bitch has been ringing and texting me all day. She's saying she wants me to pick her up."
Ali:	"Give me her number then you muppet [idiot], I'll link [meet] her then."
Kamran:	"Fuck you, you don't want her number, you won't know what to do you dopey bastard." [Laughs]
Ali:	"Show me a pic [picture] of her. Bet she's a right stinker [ugly] cuz that's all you ever get." [Laughs]

It seemed that there existed a strong sense of competition among The Boys about who was able to date the most attractive women. This is highlighted in the conversation above between Kamran and Ali, in which some of The Boys try to undermine others by telling them that the girl they were seeing or were messaging was not very attractive and that they could do better. Meanwhile, due their relationships with white British girls, a number of The Boys had children. However, the startling aspect was that these children in most cases were a well-kept secret, with The Boys not wanting their parents or the extended community to find out about them.

Children outside of wedlock were kept secret

Due to relationships with white British women, a number of The Boys had children outside of wedlock, as we discuss now. Ahmed was one of a number of boys who had a child with an ex-girlfriend. His ex-girlfriend had recently moved away from Bradford and would, from time to time, depending on how well she was getting on with Ahmed, send him pictures of his son. This became apparent when we were standing by his car one evening and Ahmed received a message on his phone. It was a picture of his son. Ahmed told The Boys:

> "Look at him; he looks a spitting image of me, look at his eyes, look bang on like mine. I bet you anything he's gonna know who his dad is when he grows up. I told her she can do what she wants, but one thing she can't do is change his dad."

Bash also had a daughter with an ex-girlfriend and, like Ahmed, was not getting on with his ex-girlfriend. Although she lived nearby, she had a restraining order on him, which restricted him from having any contact with his daughter. This was something that Bash would frequently speak about, telling The Boys how he felt disgusted with the games that his ex-girlfriend was playing in trying to prevent him from having any contact with his daughter:

> "She thinks she's fucking clever. She made out I was dangerous and that. She told the court that I was smoking bud [cannabis] around the baby and I used to smash the house up. She's full of shit: I didn't do anything, it's only because she's shagging someone else now and don't want me in her life."

Similarly, Jameel had a child with a previous girlfriend but in his case he chose not to have any relationship with his child. This became apparent when we were sitting at Bash's flat one evening and The Boys were discussing some of their past relationships with girls. Ahmed talked about a particular girl whom he referred to as being 'madly in love with him', having bought him a gold necklace, when Jameel spoke of what happened when his mother and father found out that he had a child:

> "I came downstairs and me dad was going through my phone, I forgot to lock it. He seen some pictures of me daughter and went fucking nuts. He told me mum and she was asking me who's this so I told her, I told her it's my daughter. They were, like, you have to get married, this is not allowed in Islam but I told them I'm not ready yet. I told them I'm not getting married till I'm 30."

The Boys were fully aware that relationships with girls outside of wedlock were frowned on by their parents and by the wider Pakistani community. Consequently, they would try and keep these relationships and children that they had as secret as possible, but, as highlighted in Jameel's case, this proved to be challenging. Having said this, what was interesting to learn was that while The Boys were disreputable themselves, they were at the same time unwilling to see any of their behaviour badly affecting their families. This would mean that The Boys were cautious not to be seen by the elders or by family members with the women who they from time to time would hang out with, conscious that this could be damaging for their family's *Izzat* [honour]. Research has highlighted how young Pakistani men and women are socialised from a young age to sustain the family's *Izzat* by refraining from actions that could jeopardise it (Bradby, 2007).

In the case of Salman, he was getting married soon, although an exact date for the wedding had not yet been set. The Boys would often talk about Salman's wedding and discuss which cars they would hire for the week of the wedding. The wedding was according to Pakistani traditions, with Salman getting married to a girl who his parents had arranged for him to marry. As a result of the wedding, Salman was cautious that he was not seen with another girl when hanging out with The Boys, aware that if this was ever the case then it could potentially tarnish his reputation and even damage his marriage prospects. The idea that a groom may possibly have any taint to his good name would be sufficient for the family of the potential bride to call off negotiations. Such an action would lower the status and stain the honour and reputation of the groom and his wider family. That being the case, the groom has to be seen in a positive light, and so there was considerable pressure on Salman to ensure that there was no hitch and no glitch on his character.

Not yet ready to get married in arranged marriages

As mentioned, there were cultural pressures on The Boys to get married in arranged marriages. A number of them, however, did not want to get married.

Such was the case with Afzal. His family had been trying to convince him to get married in an arranged marriage, hoping that marriage would help make him become more responsible, but as Afzal explained to The Boys one day, he wanted to enjoy his life as a single man before getting married. Ahmed also felt pressure from his family to get married – his family wanted him to marry a distant cousin – but he made it clear that he did not find the girl in the slightest bit attractive, as he humorously explained to The Boys:

> "Me mum was saying to me last night that I should get married. She said that I should marry this girl from Birmingham, one of our cousins, but boy, I can't. Should have seen her, she's proper fat, she came to my house this one time and she looked proper massive, girl needs to be on a diet for a year to lose any weight [laughing]. I was, like, Mum is there something wrong with your eyesight?"

The Boys felt that, in the eyes of the parental generation, it was often a matter of dynastic politics with the view that marriage brought two related families together, not a matter of a couple in love. This was something that Shaf was unable to comprehend, and he spoke about it one day:

> "I don't think my parents understand. They think it's OK to marry someone just because they think her parents are nice people. That don't mean shit though, they [parents] don't know what the girl is like, you don't really find out what anyone is like till you live with them."

The Boys felt that another reason why their parents wanted them to get married was because they hoped it would help them desist from criminality, this highlighting the argument that marriage has the potential to help offenders desist from criminality (Sampson and Laub, 1993, 2003). It appeared that, for some of the Marginal Boys, marriage did encourage them to desist from offending behaviours, as was the case with Mehmood and Tanny, who no longer offended. However, in the case of others, marriage did not help. If anything, it seemed that an arranged marriage led to further difficulties in their life, as was the case with Ali, who was married but separated and in the process of getting a divorce. Ali, however, continued to be involved with drugs and it seemed that his marriage had created a distance between him and his parents, with him blaming his parents for pushing him into a marriage with a girl who he later found he had little in common with. This experience left Ali feeling adamant that he would never get married in an arranged marriage again but instead would wait until he found someone suitable for himself:

> "There's no fucking way I'm doing getting married again. I knew I shouldn't – I didn't even know her and then I'm living with her. The thing is I knew straight after marriage that she's not on my wavelength, but then I thought that I do it as my mum was asking me to get married."

While the particular cultural practices discussed here were, in the eyes of The Boys, annoying and painful, there were others which they were proud to maintain, such as being able to speak *apni zabaan* (in their mother tongue), as will be discussed next.

We can speak apni zabaan

Although The Boys preferred to speak in English when conversing with one another and with other youth, they would converse with the elders in *Pothwari* (Pakistani dialect). One reason for this was because many of the elders were not fluent in English.

If any of The Boys were unable to speak Pothwari then they would not readily admit it to the others as it would be seen to be embarrassing by their peers. This was to become apparent when I was with Wahid, Yass and Ilyas one day. We were chatting away on the streets when an elderly Pakistani lady stopped to ask Yass in *Pothwari* how his mum was doing, as she had heard that his (Yass's) mum had not been well recently. In his attempt to reply to her and tell her that his mother was feeling better, Yass struggled to make himself clear which meant the lady was forced to ask him to repeat himself. Wahid and Ilyas, who were stood next to Yass, were unable to hold back their laughter, and, once the lady had walked off, started mocking Yass:

> *Ilyas*: "You can't even speak *apni zabaan* [our language] properly you muppet [idiot]. You should listen to mine, I can speak it miles better than you."

Yass, who disliked being spoken to in this way: "I can speak it better than you, you twat [idiot]."

For The Boys *Pothwari* was their second language, whereas for the elders *Pothwari* was their first and, in some cases only, language. This created conditions for confusion and mutual frustration when trying to express themselves when communicating with some of the elders. It is interesting to point out that, although The Boys and The Kids rarely spoke *Pothwari* with one another, they would habitually use words from *Pothwari* when speaking in English. This could range from the odd word or sometimes even complete sentences in *Pothwari* before resuming the conversation in English.

Having said this, what was particularly interesting to learn was that whenever any of The Boys and The Kids spoke about sensitive subjects then they would use *Pothwari* terminology. For example, if ever they spoke about drugs then it was normal of them to refer to them using words from *Pothwari* instead of the English terms. It might be more accurate to say that The Boys and The Kids developed a continuous patois of their own, sliding between formal English, colloquial street English and *Pothwari*. They would regularly greet each other as *yaar* or mate, speak to elders as *chacha* or uncle and would refer to people close to them as *bhai* [brother], and in English would refer to people as their cousin or brother. This was all done unselfconsciously, meaning that outsiders would have difficulty following what they were saying and those who only spoke English would find it extremely difficult to follow what was being said. Although this was clearly deliberate regarding illicit activities, it was not particularly deliberate regarding other relationships and activities. Some of the language was clearly inherited from tradition: for example, referring to older people as *chacha* did not always denote kinship, but did denote the tradition of respect from younger adults to older ones. Just as they sustained some traditional attitudes, The Boys modelled themselves on some of their own predecessors who had been born in the UK, and who were making adjustment to being inheritors of a traditional culture but at the same time having to adjust to a Western one.

We don't like 'back home'

Like so many other British Pakistani youth living in the UK, The Boys referred to Pakistan as 'back home'. However, what was interesting to know was that The Boys and The Kids were all born and raised in Bradford and had never really lived in Pakistan, other than for short visits for holidays, which left me wondering why they then referred to Pakistan as 'back home'.

One reason why the young men in the study referred to Pakistani as 'back home' was because of parental influence. The initial Pakistani migrants who arrived in the UK had planned on returning to their homeland after working here (Bolognani, 2009). This terminology, however, continued over the years with second- and third-generation Pakistanis continuing to refer to Pakistan as 'back home' despite having no intention of wanting to ever live in Pakistan. If anything, what was surprising to hear was that the young men in the study did not seem particularly keen on visiting what they referred to as 'back home' as we shall see.

It was to become apparent through discussion with and observation of The Boys that they really did not enjoy their visits to Pakistan. One evening as we were sitting in Bash's flat, Ahmed walked in and started telling The Boys that he may possibly be travelling to Pakistan in a few weeks' time. He explained to The Boys that his father had asked him to accompany him on what was a business trip as his father intended building a *Koti* (a large house) in Pakistan. However, Ahmed appeared somewhat uncertain as to whether he should go or not. He explained to The Boys that the last time he had visited Pakistan was when he was a child and he could barely remember what the country was like. Bash, who rarely ever kept his opinions to himself, bluntly told Ahmed that he should avoid going, explaining to him:

> "Bro, its crap out there. When I went last I couldn't stand the people, they were proper corrupt, all they wanted was my fucking money, even my cousins were playing snide games with me. They were, like, we need money, we haven't got much like you lot, we have to borrow off people. *Kasam se* [honestly] you'll regret it, time drags like fuck when you're there and you just can't wait to come back here."

As Bash's comment highlights, despite The Boys having close relatives living in Pakistan, some of them felt that their relatives were trying to use them for their money. Corruption and poverty were, in the view of The Boys, widespread in Pakistan and they were well aware that even they could fall victim to corruption. This was highlighted by Shaf who spoke of driving a hired car when he was last in Pakistan and how the police stopped him for no given reason and then demanded that he pay them before they allowed him to continue driving:

"I was coming back from Islamabad and the cops flashed me to stop and then this copper comes over to my car. He's, like, you're from England, I said yeah, why, what's that got to do with anything, why you stopped me? He tells me my lights aren't working properly and says I pay a fine, I was like what the fuck, they [lights] working, I just checked before I set off. He asks me if I want to go, I said yeah and he says I have to pay him 1,000 rupees. I said fuck me for what but then I just paid him because I knew he would just waste my time."

As highlighted by Shaf's comment, for anything to be achieved in Pakistan, The Boys felt that they had to pay bribes, but this also highlights an interesting point. For the elders, Pakistan nominally adhered to traditional values. There was no obvious promiscuity and there were theoretical harsh penalties for crime, as family values dominated. Therefore the elders were often blind to the negative side to the current Pakistani culture, recalling it as they believed it had been in their youth. But Pakistan requires payment, for example, for health care, and has no real welfare system, nor any free education, and in the tradition of only appreciating something when you no longer have it, many of The Boys came to realise that, although Britain was a tough place to live, it was in many ways preferable to any extended stay in Pakistan, in their perception. This was made apparent when Shaf returned from Pakistan in the third year of the study and made it known to the others how much he had disliked it: "You know when I got off at Manchester [airport] I felt like I was home, away from all them lot. There's no peace back there, you can't go anywhere without being hassled, they see nothing but money and they see us lot as having bare coin [plenty of money]."

While in Pakistan, some of The Boys recalled meeting lads who lived in Bradford and who were on holiday, and some who were on the run from the British police and were now residing permanently in Pakistan. On his return from Pakistan, Shaf also spoke of having 'chilled' [spent time] with someone who The Boys knew and who was on the run from the British police. The Boys were keen to find out from Shaf how this particular individual was doing:

"He [the person on the run from the police] was looking proper weak – he's stopped training out there, see. He was looking a bit stressed out, to be honest. He was telling me that he really wants to come back, he don't like it out there one bit but the thing is, he knows if he comes back then he's gonna be doing a hefty [long] sentence."

This illustrates a surprising insight into The Boys. While they were painfully aware of the problems and negative aspects of life in Britain in general and in particular in Manningham, they also found that life in Pakistan was often uncomfortable, if not hostile, in a surprising and different way. They discovered how they were homesick for Manningham and their mates and that their cousins in Pakistan often did not perceive them as Pakistanis but saw them as British Pakistanis (the 'British' coming before being the 'Pakistani'), and were sometimes hostile and often exploitative towards them. The cousins in Pakistan often seemed to have fantasies about the degree of the wealth of The Boys in the UK and expected to be subsidised from the wealth which it was assumed that the British Pakistanis possessed. As Bash highlighted earlier, "all they want is my fucking money." This exposes a profound ambivalence regarding relationships with Pakistan, and, although The Boys were living in poverty in the UK, they were shocked to see the greater extremes of poverty in Pakistan.

Relationship with Islam

This section will explore the relationship The Boys had with Islamic faith and the reason for doing so is because, as Quraishi (2005) and several other commentators have noted, criminological studies have failed to explore the religious identities of young Muslim men who offend. Another reason for exploring the relationship The Boys had with their faith was because of concerns heard that Islam, or in particular Islamic interpretations, can encourage Muslims to break the law and justify their law-breaking behaviour (see also Macey, 1999; Spalek, 2002a; Pargeter, 2006; Wahidin, 2009).

From the very outset of the study, it quickly became apparent to me that The Boys considered Islamic faith to be an immensely important facet of their life, much more important than their Pakistani ethnicity and their British nationality. The Boys would frequently make it known that they were Muslims first, then British Pakistanis after, and my findings echo those of a number of other research studies in which second- and third-generation Muslims have been found to increasingly define themselves through their religion and not their parental country of origin or nationality (for example, Shaw, 1994; Modood, 1997; Archer, 2003: Alam and Husband, 2006).

It was common to hear The Boys talk extensively about Islamic faith while hanging out. These discussions were around a variety of subjects, sometimes around theological arguments with The Boys conversing over aspects of Islam which they seemed to question. As was the time when some of The Boys discussed whether Prophet Muhammad was able to hear their prayers, an issue which Salman disagreed on and made clear to the others that such a belief went against the Islamic belief as he felt that it was only Allah who was all-hearing and all-seeing. At other times The Boys would talk around the importance of faith to their identity, while at other times these discussions were around atrocities, in particular the killings of Muslims around the world. The Boys kept a close eye on world events, above all those which involved Muslims. There was a sense of brotherhood among The Boys, a feeling that those who were being persecuted were brothers and sisters of all Muslims. Jameel and Bilal were two of several Boys who were particularly interested in what went on, and during the course of the fieldwork would speak about incidents involving Muslims. On our return from the gym one day, Jameel (who was sitting in the car), was watching a video that he had been sent on his phone by another friend. He told Bash and Ahmed about the video and how he was appalled with what he had seen: "This is a sickening clip man. They grab hold of this guy who they think is on the other side and they chop his neck off. Pure evil man, they've gone fucking nuts out there."

The newly formed terrorist group known as ISIS in Iraq was clearly disturbing for many of The Boys. The atrocities that they were committing in the name of Islam horrified The Boys so much so that they questioned whether this group were really Muslims or not. Afzal: "They [ISIS] can't be Muslims. Have you seen the shit they doing out there, killing people for fun. They are evil bastards."

Meanwhile, some of the discussions that The Boys would have on Islamic faith during the study revolved around aspects of Islam which they themselves were often unsure about and wanted to learn more about. There was one particular occasion when Ali, Nav and Ahmed, along with Shah's girlfriend, were sitting in her flat smoking cannabis when Nav started telling The Boys of how a Muslim man he knew who lived locally had recently got married again while continuing to be married to his first wife. Nav asked Ali and Ahmed how this was permissible in Islam. Ali took it on himself to try and explain to Nav the reasons why it was permissible for Muslim men to get married more than once:

Ali: "It's not as if you can get married again just for sex and that, it's got to be for a good reason to do it [get married again], and the thing is you have to ask your first wife for permission. The main thing also is that you have to treat them both equally."

Ali's response led to a disagreement, with Nav questioning how it was possible for a man who was married to two women at the same time to treat both his wives equally: "What if you prefer one [wife] more than the other, like you fancy one more than the other? How can you then treat them both the same?"

Shah's girlfriend, unable to resist having her view heard, asked Ali why it was the case in Islam that Muslim men were allowed to marry more than once when Muslim women were not. Ali clearly stumbled: he was unable to provide a convincing argument, so he undertook to ask someone else who was more learned than him in Islam and then get back to Shah's girlfriend with a convincing answer.

This conversation demonstrated how The Boys would talk about Islam frequently. Even when they were under the influence of drugs Islam remained a popular topic of conversation. However, this of course also raised the question of how The Boys could consider Islamic faith to be important to them and yet at the same time continue to offend, sell drugs and womanise? This was an aspect of The Boys' relationship with Islam which appeared most troubling and we discuss this next.

How can Islam be important when they offend?

One of the peculiar aspects of The Boys' claim that Islam was important to them was the question, why did they then continue to offend? This section consequently examines what role Islam played in the offending of The Boys, examining whether or not Islam was even used by The Boys as a motivating factor for their involvement in criminality.

It was interesting to learn that although The Boys considered Islamic faith to be an important facet of their life, they appeared fully aware that their behaviours most of the time were far from what they considered as being religious. This became apparent when we were cruising in the car one evening and The Boys began talking about Islam. The conversation had started after they had stopped to talk with a local friend who, according to them, had once been a drug dealer but now desisted from crime and was a devout Muslim. The conversation with their friend inspired The Boys to talk of how their actions were in contradiction of Islamic teachings:

Ali: "Allah has made it clear in the Quran that he curses those who sell alcohol and drink. There's going to be big punishment in the grave for us lot, eh?"

Salman: "Yeah, I know, it's going to be hard for us lot. Look how much crap we get involved in, all of these sins we have, we don't even know, but we sinning all the time, doing all this bad stuff."

It became apparent through conversation and observation with The Boys during the course of the study that, despite them being involved in a range of offending behaviour and not practising their faith by praying regularly or fasting in the holy month of Ramadan, The Boys, nonetheless in their own strange way, were religious, but their religiosity was contrasting to that of the elders or of the other Muslims living in the neighbourhood. The Boys, one could argue, were selective as to which of Islam's teachings they adhered and to which they did not want to adhere. Through observation, it became apparent that there were clearly certain Islamic teachings which they would take more seriously: for example, The Boys all abided by Islam's dietary requirements by refraining from eating pork and ensuring that the meat they consumed was only *halal*.[2] This was to become apparent when we were cruising around one evening, The Boys were talking about prison, Bash bragging to the others about how he was much more muscular when he was inside. He told them how he spent a considerable time in the gym and, because he knew an inmate who worked behind the servery, he would have extra portions of food. Ali, aware of the challenges that some Muslims faced with eating *halal* meat inside, asked Bash if he had ever eaten *haraam* food [either pork or food that was not *halal*] when he was in prison, to which Bash, in a rather aggressive manner, replied: "What the fuck do you think I am, bro? I wouldn't fucking dare eat *haraam*. If there was no *halal* food I'd stick to fish, I wouldn't dare touch pork and that, wouldn't eat it if man's paid me."

Although I had spent considerable amount of time by this stage with The Boys and felt that I knew Bash and the other boys well, I was surprised to see how strict The Boys were when it came to Islamic dietary requirements. One would have expected that, given the fact that The Boys did not pray regularly, drank alcohol and used drugs, they would not abide by Islam's dietary requirements, but this was not the case. The Boys would try and ensure they only consumed meat which was *halal* even when there were times when finding it could prove to be challenging, as highlighted in that conversation between Bash and Ali.

Another way that it became apparent over the course of the study that The Boys strictly abided by certain Islamic teachings was when, one afternoon in the gym, Salman took off his t-shirt to show Ahmed his muscular physique and in doing so Ahmed noticed that he had not shaved the hair under his armpits. "You dirty bastard, you need to shave them pits of yours," shouted Ahmed to Salman, proudly showing off his own cleanly shaved armpits. According to Islamic faith, one should shave pubic hair and hair from under the arms, and this incident clearly demonstrated how The Boys abided by this particular teaching. There were a number of other ways during the study from which I had established that Islamic faith did really mean a lot to The Boys. There were occasions when if the *Azaan* [call to prayer] could be heard coming from the local mosque, The Boys would halt conversation and listen to it until it finished before resuming conversation. The Boys, it seemed, would pick and choose which Islamic teachings they abided by. It was as if they wanted to be strict Muslims but because of their lifestyles found it difficult and, therefore, tried to abide by some Islamic teachings while neglecting others. It seemed that Islam served many different functions for them. It seemed to provide them with a sense of purpose and structure while also giving them a sense of solidarity and dignity that they felt deprived of in mainstream life.

We hope to become better Muslims one day

Although The Boys did not practise their faith in what can be referred to as the conservative way and were selective as to which of Islam's teachings they abided by, some of them did, however, express a desire to one day become better Muslims by refraining from indulging in *haraam*.

It had become apparent to me over the course of the study that, although The Boys indulged in illegal activities and rarely went to the mosque, Islam was immensely important to them. It was also not unusual for them to find their attention turned to religious matters at moments of crisis, the most frequent of which would be incarceration. Given the opportunity to reflect on their religion and the space to begin the rigorous practice of five daily prayers, The Boys could begin to challenge their own habitual behaviours – their lechery, drunkenness and drug use. Islam offered them a better, cleaner, life. As discussed in Chapter Five, what was begun in prison would sometimes fall apart on release when old habits returned, but as The Boys aged and their circumstances changed, so there were better prospects for this transformative effect to endure. Similarly, in some cases individuals such as Jameel would gradually move deeper into Islam, finding it provided everything his life on the streets and involvement in crime failed to do. He was dissatisfied with the emptiness of that life, and it gave depth and meaning to him, as to others. There was an occasion during the study when a particular incident left The Boys incredibly upset, for someone they knew and with whom they were friendly had passed away. The death of their friend had a detrimental impact on The Boys with many of them speaking about their friend and some of their memories of him.

The death of their friend greatly affected The Boys. They were fearful of what would happen to them when they died. The Islamic belief, similar to the other Abrahamic faiths, decrees that when someone dies he or she will be held to account for what they did in this world. This obviously worried The Boys, as they were aware that most of what they did was sinful. Ahmed, stood outside the mosque after the funeral prayer, clearly very emotional, telling the others how he wanted to change his life around and try and become a better Muslim:

> "I ain't doing nothing bad anymore. What is life? It's like, you're here one minute, then you're gone and then when you're in your grave, you've got to answer all them questions. I don't want to do anything wrong. I jus' wanna live a simple and good life and be there for my parents now."

The day after the death of their friend was the funeral prayer and, in accordance with the Muslim faith, the deceased was buried as soon as possible. The funeral was held in the local mosque and The Boys were all present. It was the only time during the study that I had seen every single one of The Boys all in the same place: the core, the marginal group and The Kids were all present in the mosque, having turned up to show their respects to the family of their friend. After the funeral prayer The Boys helped carry the coffin and accompanied it to the graveyard, where they helped with the burial. I was astonished to see just how apologetic they were to their friend's brother and father, for never had I seen The Boys so serious, and so supportive.

The death of their friend changed The Boys. Over the next couple of days some of The Boys were praying a lot more, and some were spending most of their time at the local mosque where people would come to show their respect to the family of the deceased. There were several visits to the graveyard where their friend was buried and where they would pray. It was as though The Boys lives had changed.

Ali and Jameel were praying a lot more after the death, Jameel telling the others while they were at the grave yard one day that: "Every soul is going to taste death, no matter how big and strong they are, and you ain't going to take anything with you, no money, nothing, it's only your good deeds that are going to go with you."

While most of The Boys went back to their old ways a week or so after the death of their friend, Jameel was different. He had become more devoted to his faith after the death and would attend mosque more regularly. There were even a number of occasions after their friend's death when, instead of hanging out with The Boys, Jameel decided to attend *Zikr* (a form of meditation) which was held in the local mosque.

An aspect of Islam that is often missed in other forms of research is the potential it has to help Muslim offenders desist from offending behaviours. As highlighted in the case of Jameel, Islam was the reason why he was now gradually moving away from offending and desisting from criminal behaviours. Meanwhile a further aspect of the relationship The Boys had with Islam was the feeling that Islam and Muslims were being almost constantly targeted by the mainstream media. The Boys would often speak about this, saying how it was causing great difficulties in their lives, as we shall discuss now.

The British media promotes hatred towards Muslims

The Boys held an adverse perception of the media. While they kept a close eye on what was going on in the world, particularly on incidents involving fellow Muslims, at the same time they felt that the British media was outright biased, and was constantly trying to give Muslims and Islam a bad image. To The Boys, this was an attack on their identity and on the things that they considered important.

Research has documented how media images have contributed to stereotyping and moral panics pertaining to Muslims (Runnymede Trust, 1997). It is noted how criminological theories about media deviancy amplification, labelling and self-fulfilling prophecies provide meaningful explanations for the emergence of the Muslim as the latest folk-devil (Runnymede Trust, 1997; Webster, 1997a; Allen, 2010; Baker, 2010; Poole and Richardson, 2006; Hargreaves, 2014). The Boys felt that negative misrepresentation of their faith by the media was partially the reason why they, too, were considered dangerous by many non-Muslims. This was to become apparent when we were sitting in Bash's flat chilling out one evening when Shaf started telling the others of an incident earlier in the day in which a white woman appeared scared of him. He explained that he had been walking down the road when a white lady, seeing him approaching her, crossed over to the other side of the road so as to avoid him. Shaf was convinced that the only reason behind her wanting to avoid him was because he was Muslim and she was scared of Muslims. On hearing what Shaf had to say, Salman spoke of a similar incident, telling The Boys of what happened when he was on the bus once:

> "I swear these fuckers are proper scared that we're gonna blow them up or summat [something]. I remember I was on the bus coming back from town as I'd been to the gym and this old *goree* [white female] was sat on the other side to me, she kept her fucking eyes on me all the way until I got off. It was like I was gonna do something to her. They're fucking paranoid to fuck, it's because of what they read in the papers, its fucked their heads up. They think we're all terrorists or summat."

Another occasion during the study when The Boys spoke extensively of the media's biased reporting towards Muslims was after the murder of Lee Rigby. They felt that the murder of Lee Rigby would be used by the British media to create further hostility and hatred of Muslims by mainstream society. A few days after the incident, The Boys were frequently speaking about how the murder of Lee Rigby by two Muslim men had left them profoundly apprehensive because they felt that it would compound the hostility of the general public towards them. In The Boys' perception, the media failed to differentiate between unrepresentative, extreme and psychotic behaviour and the religion in which they claimed to carry out such an atrocity.

The Boys were well aware of the imminent risk to themselves and their community that such hate-mongering and inaccurate, biased reporting would pose. Although it might be an exaggeration to describe their response as actually fearful, it certainly was conspicuously apprehensive. The Boys were conscious of the unpredictable probability of revenge attacks especially on 'soft' targets, such as women who would be easily identified as Muslim because of their dress, as they felt that the attack on Lee Rigby gave spurious credibility to the arguments put forward by white racist organisations, and in the eyes of the unreflective and uneducated general public. A number of stories in which Muslims had been targeted had already circulated throughout their neighbourhood.

The Boys were talking one evening about the murder of Lee Rigby and its implications on fellow Muslims:

Tanny: "I bet ya it's gonna be proper bad for Muslims now, cuz if you look you see that already so many white people don't like Muslims because of the riots [Bradford Riots] and, like, because of 9/11 and the ones in London and now you got this new one. This will see more and more Muslims get attacked, watch. I know we're lucky in Bradford, cuz there's loads of *apnas* [Muslims] so you don't get white people coming around and attacking us, but if you go to places like Newcastle or Liverpool then there's a different story."

Salman: "I know you're right, bro. You see Muslim girls getting attacked because they wear the hijab [headscarf]. Some have even had their hijabs ripped off by white racist fuckers. Believe me, I think that things are gonna get worse for us now. I don't know why these two fuckers killed the soldier but I know one thing, that things are gonna get proper bad for Muslims now."

There was a feeling of disgust among The Boys at what two Muslim men did to Lee Rigby. Many of The Boys could not understand how some Muslims could justify going around killing innocent people, and more particular doing so in the name of Islam:

Ali: "Its fucking crazy what happened. I can't believe how the fuck someone can do shit like this and what's worse, say that it was in the name of Islam. How the fuck is this in the name of Islam cuz, you know, Islam is a peaceful religion and, you know, the word Islam means peace? So how the fuck can mans go around killing innocent people? Mans just get brainwashed and they don't know what they're doing. They think they gonna go to heaven but they're wrong cuz it says in the Quran that if you kill one person then it's like killing everyone."

Another aspect of the news reporting was The Boys' feeling that very little media attention was given to people of other religions who had murdered innocent people, and yet in Britain the implication of the murder of Lee Rigby was that all Muslims were potential murderers. They felt that the murder of Lee Rigby was having all the attention, with other killings across the world, those in which innocent Muslims were dying, going unnoticed:

> *Tanny*: "There's no equality in this world. You got people dying every day in Afghanistan and Iraq, I mean innocent people dying and no one gives a fuck, and then you got one soldier who died here and everyone is making a big hoo-ha about it. You know, I'm not saying that what happened here was right, but what about the Muslims dying in Palestine, in Iraq and no one talks about them, eh?"

The Boys felt that there was selective reporting in the media. They felt injustices perpetrated against Muslims, whether in the UK or elsewhere in the world, were either not reported at all, or under-reported proportionate to the scale of the injustice experienced. They felt that attacks on mosques and on fellow Muslims in the UK were overlooked in the media, and this fuelled frustration, anger and resentment.

The Boys also felt that no matter how often Muslim leaders denounced so-called 'extremism' and 'terrorism', the media would overlook and turn a deaf ear to such denunciations, and would prefer instead to insinuate at best – and at worst, outright state – that Islam was a violent religion. They felt that the media continued to state that the atrocities carried out in the name of Islam were typical of the religion and no attempt was made to differentiate between types of Islam. As stated elsewhere, this response is especially clear when contrasted with the coverage of the 'The Troubles' in Northern Ireland. The Boys felt that there was no attempt to tarnish all Christians as terrorists following on from the bombing campaigns there, and yet there was a clear and unmistakable attempt, in their eyes, to tarnish all Muslims on the basis of unrepresentative behaviours. This, in The Boys' eyes, had the potential to create greater alienation and radicalisation by virtue of such systematic and persistent dishonesty and unfairness in media coverage.

Conclusion

The relationship The Boys have with Islam is profoundly complex and deserves further study, for not only does being a Muslim make them more tolerated by the general community (along the lines that they can't all be bad because they attend the mosque), but, on reflection, Islam often causes The Boys to question their own lifestyles. For some, the combination of Islam with the uncertainties of life have led to developing their observance of religious customs, and some, like Jameel, are in the process of successfully becoming dedicated to their religious lives, gradually turning their back on crime. For others, this is clearly a journey they are on which, combined with the slowing down brought about by age, may, and probably will, result in the same conclusion.

For The Boys life was especially difficult, as has been described. In every direction there were tensions pulling at them destructively. In their religion they had, as do all Muslims, to attempt to understand how to perceive their faith in a rapidly changing world, whether or not they sought to live out their faith wholly or eclectically. In the neighbourhood the advantages of solidarity also created the problem of restricting opportunities to leave in pursuit of a better life elsewhere, supposing that formally uneducated men with no officially recognisable professional or trade skills would be able to find remunerative work. With regard to their families, the myth of return to Pakistan had faded for their parents, but even though it had faded it still exerted a considerable hold over them – reflected in the use of the word 'home' to refer to Pakistan. However, as The Boys grew remote from the Pakistani aspect of their identification as British Pakistani, they remained deeply committed to their identification as Muslim. No matter how flawed The Boys were at implementing their beliefs and how limited their understanding of their faith was, they still remained deeply committed. Islam gave them a local and global identity and provided a code, a guide, a sense of purpose and a consolation for the vicissitudes of their hard lives. It was of utmost importance to them, even when not consciously at the forefront of their minds, and awareness of it was quickly and easily awoken especially through adversity.

Notes

[1] A Pakistani tradition of mourning the loss of a family member, men and women gather separately to pay their respects to the family of those who have lost a family member.

[2] *Halal* meat is that which is considered permissible for Muslims to eat and *haraam* is meat which Muslims are not allowed to consume.

SEVEN

Findings and conclusions

Given the increasing concern and anxiety surrounding the offending of young British Pakistani Muslim men this book has aimed to understand the lives of a particular social group of young British-born Pakistani Muslim men who were involved in a range of offending behaviours. Over the course of the study's four years, a number of themes emerged, which have been presented in this book.

This chapter discusses some of the broader difficulties that were experienced by the young men and which could explain their offending. The chapter starts, however, by discussing how, a transition was observed among many of The Boys during the study. Although towards the end of the study they were continuing to spend time socialising with one another, some were now doing so less frequently. This was almost certainly because as they grew older events such as getting married or starting a family impacted significantly on their outlook.

Some were now spending less time socialising with The Boys

A number of The Boys were now spending less of their time socialising. This was certainly the case for Bash who was in a relationship and his girlfriend was also pregnant. Salman was another who towards the latter stages of the study was spending less of his time with The Boys. In his case, the reason was because he was getting married and was now helping his family plan his wedding.

In contrast with the start of the study when Jameel would present himself as someone not to be messed with, his behaviour had changed considerably over the course of the study. He was much calmer, and this was almost certainly due to his new-found devotion to the Islamic faith. Jameel was now trying to balance devotion to Islamic faith along with socialising with The Boys. He would attend the mosque daily and was also now regularly attending a weekly meditation class (also known as *Zikr*). However, one had to wonder how long it would be possible for Jameel to balance street life with devotion to Islamic faith, a task that would be immensely difficult, given the lifestyles of The Boys.

Several of The Boys were exploring the idea of starting up in business: Ali, for example, was considering the possibility of going into a legal business venture. It was interesting to note that a number of The Boys now saw business as a way of making money legally without having to constantly look over their shoulders to see if the police were on their case. However, in order to set up in business, substantial savings were required, which, of course, The Boys did not have at present and this would see some of them continuing to pursue a drugs career with a view of one day acquiring the necessary monies to go into legal avenues, as was the case with Ali. But things do not always go according to plan, and for now Ali was still involved in drugs and this, of course, presented a constant risk that he could at any time 'get busted' [caught by the police] and return to prison.

Some were refusing to grow up

While a number of The Boys were now showing signs of maturity and desistance, others showed no signs of any change in their behaviour. Nav, who in the past had spoken of wanting to go straight [crime free] had gradually moved away from the company of The Boys and was now hanging around with some of The Kids. This infuriated The Boys, who would often remark on how they felt that Nav's behaviour was 'too childish' for their liking. Ahmed was another of The Boys who was spending time with some of the area's younger lads. He was back with his ex-girlfriend, and this annoyed The Boys, who considered his girlfriend to be a compulsive liar (she had previously told Ahmed that she was pregnant, only for them to find out later from one of her friends that she had been lying all along).

As the study unfolded, the way in which The Boys themselves commented on Nav's and Ahmed's childish behaviour showed how they were gradually ceasing to be The Boys, slowly and imperceptibly moving into a new phase of life on the edge of being young adults and entering middle age. This was not an obvious or conscious issue with them, except insofar as their experience of getting married and starting families influenced on the way in which they socialised, but it did further explain a new outlook on their past, along the lines of 'when we were kids'. The lack of self-consciousness did not mean maturing was not happening: instead it meant that, as with so many other things in their lives, there was a level of awareness which was not analysed, but simply accepted.

The Kids were replacing The Boys, becoming more criminal, more money focused

In the case of The Kids there was, compared to when The Boys were younger, a relatively immature focus on 'mucking about' as a way of life which also legitimised criminality similar to Katz's (1988) view of crime as, at least in part, an adrenaline rush. This was changing to a more sedate view of crime as a business venture. While 'having a laugh' persisted, it was less of a dominant theme. The Kids were becoming more focused on wanting to make money: some were already involved in the sale of drugs while others were thinking of starting 'a round' [selling and delivering drugs]. Their clientele was different too. Many of The Kids saw Eastern Europeans who were moving into the area as potential customers, conversing with them, asking them if they wanted to buy any drugs – "I got *dobra* [good] thing for you" – whenever they recognised any of them.

It seemed that, as the study unfolded, The Kids were gradually coming to have more dominance on the streets, although, having said that, one aspect of The Kids' lives that the study highlighted was the level of naivety among them when going about their offending. On the whole, The Kids were not, it seemed, as shrewd as The Boys, particularly when it came to selling drugs. The principal explanation for this was that they did not have the experiences The Boys had had with the police which had made them sharper. The Kids, when going about their drug dealing, were more likely to be discovered by the police as was the case for Yass who was waiting to go back to the police station, having been arrested for possession of heroin with intent to supply.

The Kids will no doubt move on to replace The Boys and gradually become more involved with drugs, which will inevitably see them enter prison. It is worth pointing out that there is already a new, much younger group of boys who are slowly coming through on the streets and who are replacing The Kids. No doubt this younger group will go on to make some of the same mistakes as previous generations and follow in the footsteps of the older generations. And each generation, when they get older, speaks of how the younger boys are becoming more criminalised than they themselves were when they were younger. This in itself indicates a change of values between the younger and the older generation: whereas The Boys had a sense of cultural tradition and solidarity which generated cohesiveness and a sense of boundary, a code of behaviour, when dealing with each other and with others within the community of Manningham, the younger generation were moving to more individualistic and violent values. They have not, therefore, experienced the sense of community to the same degree that the older boys did.

Broader difficulties experienced by the young men in the study

A key aspect this research highlighted was the broader difficulties and challenges that were experienced by the young men. The Boys lived in areas of poverty and came from deprived households. Their fathers were either unemployed or worked in low-paid jobs, and their mothers were housewives. Merton's (1968) strain theory was consequently an attractive explanation for their offending, as Merton found that poverty had the potential to lead to a strain between the accepted goals of society and the socially approved means of reaching them. It became apparent through the course of observation and conversation with The Boys that they offended in order to reach socially approved goals which were otherwise blocked for them. There was a real desire among them to do well financially, aspiring to one day drive luxurious cars, wear expensive clothes, and even live in affluent parts of Bradford. Money was also considered a route to status in the community, having the potential of raising one's profile among their peers.

One particular factor that fuelled a desire to make money was to do with the make-up of the neighbourhood. The neighbourhood in which The Boys lived in was made up predominantly of established Pakistani residents and this in itself led to a sense of competition about wealth among its residents. There were clearly some members who were much more financially successful than others and yet who continued to live in the same community and this was because of benefits such as ethnic solidarity, living near to the mosque, *halal* shops and so on. The Boys would themselves measure who had the most wealth, and would, while hanging out, constantly talk of ways in which they could make a raise [profit], most of the time referring to making money illegally.

The severity of unemployment was a further factor adding to the attraction of criminality. Jobs were difficult to come by, and Bradford was a very different place today from how it had been when the first generation of Pakistani migrants arrived in the city, finding work in the thriving textile trade. This trade, as discussed in Chapter Two, had almost ceased to exist. It is also important to point out that The Boys, unlike the previous generation, were particularly selective in the types of employment they were prepared to undertake, with street credibility playing a role in determining which jobs they felt were suitable or not. Albert Cohen's (1955) 'status frustration theory' was another attractive explanation explaining the young men's offending. They had a lack of education, having gained little or no qualifications when they were at school. In the hope of earning status from their peers, The Boys were involved in criminal behaviour. Cohen argued that youth who offended were more likely to fail at school and would consequently feel humiliated. In an attempt to gain some sort of status among their peers, these youths would then develop subcultures which invert traditional middle-class values such as obedience, politeness and obeying the law, hoping that these inverted behaviours would provide them with status among their peers. The Boys felt a need to have status and street credibility, and to be associated with certain crimes and older boys brought with it recognition among their peers that they were 'connected' and not to be messed with.

Bradford is home

Meanwhile, another aspect of The Boys' lives that this study highlighted was their reluctance to leave the city in which they had grown up. While there was the odd conversation among some that they were planning to move away in order to try and find work, this never transpired. In reality, it would be surprising to see any of them leave Bradford. Despite the difficulties and challenges that they experienced living in Bradford, the city was considered home. It was a place they knew incredibly well and where they felt comfortable. In fact, as this study has shown, not only were The Boys uncomfortable away from Bradford, but were so even when they were away from Manningham. Part of the explanation for this was, of course, that they were born and raised in Manningham and knew the area and its residents particularly well. Other factors were to do with a dependency on their families and in particular on parents and siblings. Therefore, life away from Bradford was unthinkable.

There was also a feeling among the young men that, although Manningham was not a haven of tranquillity, it was still a much safer and much more tolerant place for Muslims to live than elsewhere in Britain. There was a feeling among The Boys that, due to terrorist attacks carried out in the name of Islam, there was a danger that Muslims could be attacked by racist individuals and groups in so-called revenge attacks. Manningham was considered safe for Muslims, and it also had mosques, *halal* butchers and grocery shops that catered for the needs of the Muslim Pakistani residents. The Boys were very aware of the increasing number of attacks on Muslims elsewhere in Britain, and of the rise of the far right with its conflation of Islamophobia and racism (Winlow et al, 2017). Bradford in general, and Manningham in particular, offered safety. It offered identity, security, tradition and continuity – which were advantages, but which restricted the opportunity to move out of the area for better job prospects. The Boys were trapped by fear, provincialism and by cultural tradition.

It was easy to become a drug dealer

As discovered in this study, many of the young men were actively involved in selling illegal drugs and one particular aspect of drug dealing that this study highlighted was the ease with which they were able to turn to drug dealing in order to try and make money. You did not even need to be a 'proper' drug dealer; you could simply act as a middleman and make money in the process. However, while it was relatively easy to become drug dealers, at the same time there was fierce competition from the more established dealers. As a result, this would see many, in particular the younger boys, take increased risks when trying to find new customers, which in return meant that they ran a greater risk of being easily detected by undercover police and consequently spending time in prison.

A further factor relating to drug dealing which this study highlighted was the extent to which peer pressure and manipulation was used by some of the older established dealers on the younger boys such as The Kids to sell drugs for them. The benefit of having younger dealers sell drugs for them was that it presented less risk of the older boys getting caught by the police. For this reason, involvement in drugs was in many ways like being faced with a double-edged sword for the younger boys – on the one hand, being pushed by older boys into being street dealers and on the other having to constantly be vigilant so to avoid getting caught by the police. There is often a lack of understanding of the path that leads so many British Pakistani young men in places like Bradford to become involved in drugs. While a way out would be for the younger dealers to inform the police of the names of those individuals who pressurised them into selling drugs, there is a need to understand that to be known as a 'snitch' within neighbourhoods like the ones the young men in the study lived in could seriously damage street credibility and potentially lead to bullying. Consequently, many of the younger dealers considered it better to pay the price and suffer the consequences if caught with drugs by the police rather than inform on the dealers whom they were working for.

Furthermore what this study has demonstrated is that the issue of drugs is far more complex than might be supposed. The variety of substances is in itself highly diverse. The skills needed to deal are highly sophisticated, despite the stigma of dealing itself. The need to find the drugs, to control quality, to find trustworthy runners, to ensure the profit margins are guaranteed, then also to be alert, not just to deceit from suppliers, runners and customers, but also entrapment and prosecution. If these skills were used in the retail of any other product then they would be lauded as benefiting the economy, and that would appear to be the key to this issue. The Boys had very highly developed entrepreneurial skills, but the direction they had taken was because of a number of reasons. Though stigmatised and regarded as outcasts by mainstream society, The Boys demonstrated many outstanding qualities: not just entrepreneurial skills but intense, if fractious, loyalty, a strong sense of duty to family and a strong, if eclectic, moral code. In many ways The Boys were admirable, although their good qualities are rarely visible to themselves and even less often visible to the outside world.

The process of labelling

While it cannot be denied that a significant proportion of drug dealers in Bradford are of Pakistani origin, this raises several significant issues. One is the way in which Pakistani ethnic identity is highlighted so prominently in the media, whereas the ethnic identity of drug dealers from other groups is not emphasised in the same way – a consequent issue is the labelling process that this involves. A further issue is the negative consequence of glamorising drug dealing in the minds of those not involved who, via the media, begin to see dealing as a high-risk but potentially extremely profitable activity in an area blighted by unemployment and severe poverty.

As highlighted in this study, the young men had a feeling of being targeted by the media and the police because of their belonging to the Pakistani ethnicity and Islamic faith. They viewed the police as having racist tendencies and of using heavy-handed tactics against them. Relationships between British Muslim communities and the police have been a cause for great concern which has been well documented (see Chakraborti, 2007; Hargreaves, 2014). A further ingredient was the perception of The Boys that the authorities single out Pakistani males for especially harsh treatment, and that white criminals guilty of the same sort of crimes are treated more leniently, a perception having some justification in the criminological evidence about different and discriminatory treatment (Bhui, 2009; Uhrig, 2016). While their actions were criminal a lot of the time and therefore punishable, the punishment and sentences handed down on The Boys were viewed as being far harsher than those given to white youth for similar crimes. This resulted in a feeling among The Boys of resentment, and they, in turn, viewed any kind of authority as deliberately targeting them, often commenting on how the police wanted to see more Muslims behind bars and how Muslims were being 'slammed' [punished harshly] by the courts. The perception of the police as frequently racist is one that, as we learned from this study, lingered among the young British Pakistani Muslims featured in it and it is crucial that this is addressed otherwise there is always a danger that Bradford runs a serious risk of a repeat of the riots of 1995 and 2001. It is important to remember that many of the young men in the study were too young to have taken part in the 2001 riots, and those who were involved in them from the Pakistani community have themselves become older. Now it is the younger generation who are eager to show their resentment against the way they are treated by the authorities.

Generational tension was evident

A further aspect of tension that this study has highlighted was the generational conflict that existed between The Boys who were born and raised here in the UK and the elders, the Pakistani parent generation who were born and raised in Pakistan.

An aspect of this intergenerational conflict was the usual problems in a developing society of the young wanting to succeed the old. This was, however, compounded by the transition and cultural adaptation necessary for a tradition which had not changed for centuries, a tradition more suited to a pre-industrial rural community than life in a highly complex developed industrial society. All the assumptions the elders took for granted had to be questioned by The Boys in the process of their adaptation. While, therefore, it is true that there has been conflict between fathers and sons since time began, there were additional elements impacting on The Boys. With changes in behaviours and in what was considered to be acceptable or not, there were, as discussed in Chapter Six, elements of Pakistani culture which The Boys found difficult to abide by: for example, having relationships outside of wedlock and consuming alcohol were forbidden by Pakistani culture, which The Boys found difficult. They were creatures of synthesis. They could not ignore the dominant society in which they lived, but they had to negotiate between secular non–Muslim society and their traditional culture, which, in some aspects, was impossible to live by in modern Britain. For The Kids, the rate of this process had accelerated, with The Boys having pioneered compromise and, so to speak, blazed a trail in acknowledging cultural tradition and religious affiliation, and yet also interacting with mainstream society. An example of this is the number of The Boys who had non-Pakistani girlfriends.

The elders had not experienced the challenges faced by the youth who were born and raised in the UK, and were oblivious of what their sons were going through. They were not able to understand the desire to have street credibility, to be known in the neighbourhood as someone not to be messed with: these were notions that were of little significance to the elders. A further factor that the study has highlighted was how the elders appeared to struggle to communicate with the youth in ways that inspired them to want to turn their lives around and stop offending. Quite simply, the young men in the study felt that the Pakistani elders were unable to understand their lives.

Further tensions with the elders were about Islam. Many of the elders encouraged the youth to abide by Islamic teachings, but in the eyes of The Boys some of the elders were ignorant of these themselves. The Boys felt that there were some elders selling alcohol within their restaurants and shops, but then telling them to refrain from drug dealing. This made little sense to them as alcohol was evidently sinful to trade according to Quranic teachings.

Another factor was the alienation felt by the young men in matters of faith, as the Imams [preachers/teachers of the faith] appeared to be remote from young British Muslims because they were mostly born and raised in Pakistan. It was felt that these Imams had little understanding of the dilemmas that were faced by young British Muslims. Mosques have become increasingly important in the issues surrounding the younger generation, with concerns that they are badly failing many of the young. It is felt they are manipulated by elders and committees instead of responding to the needs and experiences of young English-speaking, British-born Muslims. This is, of course, a contested claim, but mosques and their management are increasingly drawn into controversy. This is spectacularly compounded at present with the media's demonisation of radicalisation and the role of Imams in preventing it. In view of this, it seems likely that the leadership of mosques will continue to be the centre of attention, not just over guidance to the young, steering them away from crime, but also other activities disapproved of by the state. A superficial reading of the crime problem would suggest that this is a problem the resolution of which lies with the Pakistani and religious leaders, but this initial response may be facile and dangerous. Drugs and criminal behaviour are widespread throughout the UK among all communities, transcending ethnic, religious, class and gender boundaries. Therefore, the issue then becomes one of why, of all the communities, the Pakistani Muslim community features so prominently in prosecutions and in prisons.

They were just like any other group of boys

This study has highlighted that, despite the negative portrayal of British Pakistani Muslim men in the media, the young men in the study were just like so many others up and down the country, with similarities in traits and behaviours. They have full human identities, an aspect that is so often overlooked in discussion: when talking about Pakistani Muslim male criminals, their humanity and personal identity is often lost in sweeping generalisations and stereotyping.

Although this study has noted the importance of ethnicity and religion in the identity and mindset of The Boys, at the same time these should not be exaggerated. The Boys conformed to very British standards and perceived themselves to be British. They were born in England, they preferred to speak English when out of the home, and they were sometimes criticised by the elders for not speaking their ancestral language fluently. Their music, their food, their aspirations were all typical of their generation. On their occasional visits to Pakistan they were regarded as British and not Pakistani by their Pakistani cousins. Many of them, as discussed in Chapter Six, hated their visits to Pakistan and could not wait to return home to the UK. In most regards The Boys were simply typical of men of their generation, irrespective of ethnicity.

Despite their involvement with drugs and criminal activity, what came across very clearly throughout the study was that they had a very strong sense of morality and a particularly strong sense of loyalty, solidarity and mutual support to one another. There was a sense of honour that dominated their behaviour, albeit a profoundly masculine one. Meanwhile, one apparent puzzle that emerged was why people with such diverse attitudes would choose to socialise together and display such loyalty and cohesion. Some appeared deeply religious in their thinking, others were very secular with heavy drinking and gambling and drug habits, and yet they were bound to each other by shared community living, ties of age, ethnicity, culture and a sense of issues that superseded all possible divisions. The use of the word 'bro' among The Boys was actually a profoundly revealing and insightful piece of terminology. They were bound by a sense of kinship that transcended all divisions and endured all vicissitudes.

The Pakistani community is a community undergoing radical and rapid transition. This is often apparent when The Boys make visits to their ancestral land and discover that they are regarded as foreigners by their cousins in Pakistan. This can raise various levels of ambivalence. Not only do they feel estranged from their ancestral land, and resentful at their perception of being swindled by their cousins (who charge different prices for them than they would for resident Pakistanis), but they also feel an additional layer of resentment at the expectation of so many of their cousins living in Pakistan to have money sent to them from the UK. The misconception in Pakistan is that everyone in Britain is wealthy and can easily afford to support them, and this links also to land disputes where British Pakistanis owning land in Pakistan find that their own relatives have illegally taken that land from them. Such experiences increase the sense of alienation from Pakistan felt by British Pakistanis.

It is also apparent in their conversations with their elders (where different value systems emerge) that, on occasion, they do so confrontationally. But, for The Boys, perhaps the most startling and disturbing area where they sense that they themselves are part of a value system that is being rejected, is the changes in behaviour and belief among the girls. They had shared their parents' attitude that women were to be respected – at least Pakistani women within the community, if not other women. What they were now finding is that younger Pakistani girls want to participate in drug culture and to adopt the ways of thinking and acting which had characterised The Boys when they were younger, which they had deemed acceptable on the grounds that they were male. Some girls found it acceptable to behave violently, including fighting each other and assaulting, for example, teachers. When I visited Afzal's house I was astonished to find that two of his nieces were proud of their own records for fighting and exclusion from school for attacking a teacher. Additionally, they boasted that they smoked skunk, and sold it to their peers. They were modestly dressed in traditional Asian clothes and outwardly appeared demure. Initially I suspected that this was a fabrication and that the girls, knowing of my research interest, were lying. I was subsequently able to verify what they had told me. They said their parents were aware of their consumption of skunk, but not of other things they did. The Boys generally acknowledged that there was a growing presence of Pakistani girls in the drug culture, and that the behaviour of Pakistani girls was changing very rapidly, in many ways rejecting the traditional value of submissiveness to protective male relatives, with involvement in drugs, therefore, just part of a wider change among them.

Limitations of the study

Just like all studies, this study featured a number of limitations. One was the fact that it was conducted in a particular geographical area. While its findings can be generalised, these will, of course, depend on a number of different factors such as ethnicity, age and religion of participants.

Another limitation with the study was the danger that a researcher, who himself is a British Pakistani and has grown up in Bradford risked becoming too attached to the lives of those under study. There was the potential problem that the researcher was too close to the study, and because he was so close, he may not see things that someone who was more distant would notice, on the grounds that the observer took them for granted. However, this was counterbalanced by the fact that the observer's identity gave him access to The Boys in a way that someone of a different background may not have had: they would not have had the same level of access, nor have been trusted so much by The Boys.

A further limitation of the study was the dilemma of trying to get all the information about the lives of The Boys written in a final form so as to present it in a way which would do justice to their lives. Despite the comprehensiveness of the data obtained on the young men, and despite every effort, certain aspects of The Boys and The Kids lives will no doubt have been missed.

Final words

This study has provided a detailed insight into the lives of young men who are often spoken about and yet of whom so much remains unknown: the perspective of young Muslim men who were involved in delinquent behaviours. This book exposes the complex nature of the processes which lead to the involvement of young British Pakistani Muslim males in crime.

The study has highlighted the scarcity of research from people who have this level of access to the lives of young Muslim men who offend, who are an accepted peer rather than an outsider to be wary of, however politely that outsider is treated. There is a need for further research across a wide range of avenues, not only because statistics indicate a substantial increase in the number of young British Muslim males imprisoned, but because their profile in the UK is growing. Consequently, the question that needs to be looked at is whether the rise in offending is explained through the demography of this group, or explained through other factors (Marsh, 2006). According to Webster

(2007: 114): 'Previous studies of minority ethnic young people in the youth justice system are few, and so dated that social and demographic change may have invalidated their findings'.

A time of growing concerns of alienation by communities gives policy development a sense of extreme urgency. At the same time, boys do not stay boys, they move on, becoming older, marrying and having children. This is the stage The Boys are at now. They are slowly moving away from the tight-knit, reckless, hedonistic group of lads, and becoming the parental generation, while their place is being taken by a new generation. At the same time, a further, perhaps surprising, feature has emerged from this study. The Boys have very strong positive values. They are committed wholeheartedly to their families and uphold virtues such as loyalty. They can be easily shocked, and, notwithstanding the generalisations and stereotyping of the media, they have a very strong sense of honour and respectability. They are also highly intelligent, and in their criminality have demonstrated positive and entrepreneurial skills which, if redirected to other activities, would strongly benefit society. These are talented young men who are locked out of society.

While The Boys in this study may be written off as incorrigible criminals, it is urgent that policies are put in place to prevent this from happening to younger people. As The Boys age and desist, they are replaced by the younger and more bitter Kids whose code of behaviour and outlook on life is fiercer, and potentially more threatening.

The relentless partisan, biased and hostile coverage by certain elements of the media which equates all Pakistani men with grooming and all Muslims with extreme fanaticism breeds a sense of loathing towards Pakistani males and towards Islam among the general public which The Boys are very well aware of. This creates a siege mentality, and is compounded by their awareness of the suffering of Muslims in other parts of the world and the double standards used by so much of the media. The writings of journalists such as Katie Hopkins in *The Sun*, describing Syrian refugees as 'cockroaches' (Saul, 2015), certainly has not helped reduce any tension. For such a major outlet of the media, part of a global media empire, to feel it is acceptable to analyse a difficult political and humanitarian issue in such terms is difficult even for non-Muslims to comprehend. The incitement to hatred that comes from such intemperate and inappropriate language is clear to see. It is not surprising, in these circumstances, to see why the young men in the study have a sense of alienation from society and have developed an alternative value system to those of the 'establishment'. It would seem, on current performance, to be impossible in a liberal democracy to achieve fairness and balance in the media. It is ironic that the very same media that is so unfairly savage in its coverage of the community then complains about the community it misrepresents.

A further and internal Muslim response that would most definitely help in this regard is the creation of more Muslim leaders, community leaders and Imams who are knowledgeable about life in the West and who are able to converse with the youth and understand their situations and lives. However, many mosques in Bradford are still dominated by Urdu-speaking Imams with limited insight into the problems experienced by the young. While this is changing now, with some mosque leaders seeing the problem, there is still some way to go in providing the leadership that matches the needs of those who have to be guided and led. But at the same time, the view of many non-Muslims that it is down to the mosques to resolve all the problems is another variant of blaming the victims. Many of the problems from which young Muslims suffer are imposed on them externally, and it is undoubtedly true that those who cause the problems have a significant part to play in removing those causes and help instead to create solutions. The Boys and The Kids have a great contribution to make for the betterment of themselves and of society in general, and it is urgent that they now be enabled to do so.

What this study indicates is that, in the interests of the stability of society and the credibility of liberal values, there have to be proactive policies implemented, and led energetically and proactively by the establishment in order to counteract the entrenched perception of an increasing number of younger Muslims that society is against them, and nothing they do will earn them respect or create fair chances for them to contribute to society and benefit from it. This needs to occur alongside changes within the Muslim community ensuring better quality leadership, which is a repeated call from the establishment. It is urgent and vitally important that appropriate policies are devised, initiated and implemented from all directions in order to help young men like those in this study.

Appendix

When conducting a study wherein the researcher spends considerable time with individuals who offend, it is essential to be able to build trust and establish an atmosphere of comfort and trust with the study participants. This, as Conroy (2003) suggests, is because participants need to feel safe and confident in the knowledge that they can speak openly and frankly, knowing that there will not be any repercussions from what they say. Noaks and Wincup (2004: 43) similarly note that 'all research participants should experience an approach that gives attention to protecting their rights, seeks to achieve informed consent and respects promises of confidentiality'. The researcher was aware that in order for The Boys to cooperate with the study, they needed reassurance that the research would not result in them getting into any trouble with the law. One way of maintaining confidentiality was to reassure participants that they would remain anonymous. Throughout the study pseudonyms have been used instead of the real names of the participants. Another way of maintaining confidentiality was to make anonymous the precise area in which the young men lived. It is worth pointing out that the young men lived in a broad geographical area (Manningham) which had countless groups of young Pakistani men, many of whom had parallels in appearances and behaviours with those under study. This, the researcher felt, would help maintain the anonymity of the precise area of where the young men lived.

The exact timing of events is only reported in this study where it is integral to the unfolding account. Precise timings are avoided to preserve anonymity, although the broad sequence of events is maintained throughout. However, the researcher was also aware, as King (2000: 307) suggests, that despite every effort, 'confidentiality can never be absolute'. This is because detecting the identity of the target population and their location was not an impossible task for the trained eye.

The researcher was aware that although he knew the young men prior to conducting a phenomenological study of their lives, this did not mean that The Boys felt confident enough to trust him entirely, which meant that every effort was needed to try to build trust with the young men. One particular method that the researcher followed early on in the research to try and build trust with The Boys was to avoid asking them questions about sensitive topics such as their personal lives or their offending behaviour. To start asking questions with people in the field without first getting to know them can create awkwardness and disapproval, resulting in the researcher missing out on crucial information about the lives of those he is studying (Aspers, 2009). The researcher instead waited until The Boys became better acquainted with him and felt more at ease in his presence before asking such delicate topic-oriented questions. Bogdan and Taylor (1975: 57) note that 'there are certain questions which are too sensitive to ask, until the observer has won the confidence of subjects, and the only way for the observer to know which issues are especially sensitive is to sit back and listen'.

Another method used to earn trust and build rapport with the young Pakistani Muslim men in the study was to participate in some of the same activities that the young men were involved in. Becker's (1963: 168) advice on this is that 'the researcher must participate intensively and continuously with the deviants he wants to study so that they will get to know him well enough to be able to make some assessment of whether his activities will adversely affect theirs'. Examples of the types of activities that the researcher participated in varied over the course of the fieldwork. The most common ones were cruising in their cars, going to the gym, spending time at Bash's flat or at Shah's girlfriend's flat and occasionally visiting the mosque for Friday prayers.

It is important to point out, as Johnson (1975: 98) states, that 'trust is not a one-time phenomenon but an ongoing development process'. The researcher felt that, although trust could be earned, maintaining trust with The Boys could prove to be a completely different challenge altogether. Consequently, it was of paramount importance for him to consistently work on maintaining trust, as any breach in confidentiality could close down all communication between The Boys and himself. This could potentially create a negative snowball effect with The Boys seeing some respondents become aware of the breach and then themselves declining to cooperate any further with the study.

There were a few examples over the course of the study when the researcher felt that trust may have been brought into question with The Boys, and these are mentioned here. There was an occasion when the police turned up at Ahmed's girlfriend's house to question him in relation to a particular incident. This left Ahmed and the other boys baffled as to how the police knew who Ahmed's girlfriend was, let alone where she lived. There was another occasion when The Boys could not comprehend how the police discovered that they had drugs in the car. These incidents naturally made the researcher feel that The Boys would question whether it was him who was carrying information about them and others in the neighbourhood back to the police. However, they never said anything that warranted this feeling, nor did they behave in any way that would lead the researcher to believe that they did not trust him, so these feelings were quickly dismissed.

As for The Kids, it was only possible for the researcher to spend time with them late into the process of the fieldwork as it took time to develop the sense of trust with them. Their trust in the researcher grew derivatively from their witnessing of the trust shown by The Boys. The reasoning of The Kids was that if the researcher was acceptable to The Boys, then they too had nothing to fear or worry about, and they had no need to show caution towards the researcher.

The researcher, over the course of the study, tried his best to immerse himself in the lives of the young men by speaking with them, joking with them, empathising with them and sharing their concerns and experiences (Bogdan and Taylor, 1975), aware that it would only be through such a process that he would be able to earn their trust and understand their lives as lived by them. However, where the target group is being researched for the primary reason that it is criminal, and very little is known about it, there are serious ethical issues raised by the types of activities in which the researcher can and cannot get involved in.

Studying illegal activity as it happens

One of the main ethical concerns with a study aiming to understand the lives of individuals involved in criminal behaviour as it was lived was the need to ask pertinent and sensitive questions. Does the researcher facilitate The Boys to commit crime? Does he refrain from participating in any form of criminal behaviour, or does he leave the scene every time The Boys indulge in criminal activity? The researcher realised that whichever way he decided to go in this matter he was likely to encounter problems. If he committed a crime then his actions risked prosecution. If he chose to leave the scene every time The Boys committed a crime, he excluded himself from vital information about the young men and their lives.

The researcher made a decision to refrain from participating in criminal acts, and to follow Maguire's example of morality in his study with street criminals. Maguire (2000: 134) had an ethical challenge relating to an invitation from two known offenders to join them on a job. Such an experience made him aware of the need for setting boundaries or 'line drawing'. For Maguire, the line was drawn in such a way in order to prevent his participation in the criminal act. He acknowledges that this has to be a personal and moral decision for each individual researcher, as no one was able to speak universally – for all researchers concerned – in such a delicate matter. However, the intimate involvement of an investigator with deviant (and often illegal) activity has been seriously questioned by researchers – for example, by Yablonsky (1965: 56) who suggested that the investigator has an obligation as an upstanding and law-abiding citizen to report illegal behaviour to the proper authorities. Similarly, Polsky (1969) argued that one does not have to even participate in any offending behaviour to still be liable. This is because even studying law-breaking deviants as they engage in their deviance in the natural setting means that in some ways the researcher will break the law himself.

From the very outset, the researcher was aware that conducting a phenomenological study of the lives of a social group of young Pakistani Muslim men who offend will mean him being placed in some challenging situations – for example, merely sitting in cars that were not insured with drivers who were banned from driving. In addition, there were times when The Boys consumed a number of illegal drugs, and would encourage the researcher to join them. There were even occasions when The Boys were involved in drug dealing and would speak about their activities rather openly. Having said this, it was exceptionally difficult to confirm with certainty the full extent of their drug dealing because most of the young men went about their business in a careful and very secretive way.

All of the aforementioned situations left the researcher worried about what the outcome would be should they be stopped by the police. He was fearful, for example, that if the vehicle The Boys were in was found to have drugs onboard, then he too could be arrested. This prompted the researcher to question whether he should report involvement in criminal activity which the study participants were involved in to the police so that they were aware of why the researcher was spending time with The Boys. Berk and Adams (1970) argue that this position presents the problem of how can the investigator expect to gain the trust necessary to gather information about deviant activities if the participants know that key significant activities will be reported to the police? Informing the police about the research also carried the risk that the police would know the precise location of the research and who exactly The Boys were. For this reason the researcher decided not to inform the police of The Boys' criminal activities. The researcher was also aware that to inform the police, or even be suspected of colluding with the police, carried the potential of jeopardising the entire study, not to mention issues with confidentiality and trust.

However, it was decided that if a situation arose where the researcher was arrested, he would then inform the police of the study. It was important to this researcher that he was fully aware of the risks being undertaken, and to achieve a balance between gaining the confidence of The Boys without betraying his own moral beliefs or his legal position, so as to empower The Boys to speak for themselves. The aim was to be able to work without fear and to achieve a good piece of research, enabling the policy makers to be aware of certain key issues so that they could modify policies in a way to benefit society in general and The Boys in particular.

One way of overcoming such concerns was to leave the setting every time a crime was taking place. However, as Adler (1993: 44) in her study with drug dealers highlights, 'we were fearful of the police, we knew it was possible to get caught in a bust yet buying and selling was so pervasive that to leave every time it occurred would have been unnatural, and highly suspicious'. If a drug deal was in process, if discipline was being enforced or a dispute being resolved violently, then the idea of objectivity becomes problematic. The researcher is at risk of becoming an accessory before, during or after the fact of the crime. At the same time, any researcher using phenomenological methods who informs the police each time a criminal action takes place is clearly going to lose the confidence of the target population. The researcher may even be putting his own safety at risk, as James Patrick (1973) discovered during his cohort investigation into a gang. He was forced to leave his study fieldwork due to feeling threatened, and had to wait years before publishing his work.

The difficulties and complexities of gathering data

For research to be scientific, it requires the methodology to be as objective, reliable and as valid as possible. However, in social sciences the selection of methods used are determined by the nature of the research topic. In this particular case, the very nature of the subject – involving young British Pakistani Muslim men who were engaged in illegal activities – required great sensitivity, which affected data gathering.

Throughout the study the researcher was always open and honest with the study's participants, aware, as Adler (1993: 25) mentions, that 'ethical dilemmas are directly related to the amount of deception researchers use in gathering data, and the degree to which they have accepted such acts as necessary and therefore neutralized'. One of the key aims from the commencement of the study was to build rapport with The Boys so that the study could achieve what it had set out to achieve, with a positive effect on data gathering. Berk and Adams (1970: 113) state that 'it is generally a good idea not to become overly intent on gathering data, until acceptance by the group is clear', and argue that 'too many researchers are either over-ambitious or are limited by time, money or and patience try to gather data before rapport is established'.

Once rapport and trust had been built by the researcher, the other problem with collating data was whether the researcher should record notes in front of The Boys or when he was on his own. Bogdan and Taylor (1975: 65) comment that 'there are very few instances in which it is advisable to take notes in the field. Note taking reminds subjects that they are under constant surveillance'.

Data gathering was carried out by spending time with The Boys and making notes on returning home, writing up as much of what could be remembered of the day's events, similar to making a reflective journal entry. However, this presented the challenge of remembering to make notes after spending time in the field. There were a few occasions when, after having spent the evening with The Boys, the researcher returned home late at night and struggled to find the energy to make detailed notes of the day's events. Nonetheless, on the overwhelming number of occasions, the researcher relied on his memory to record the day's events.

In addition to making notes, one has great difficulty knowing what to record, how to record it and what to make of it (Parker, 1974). When observing and spending time with The Boys, the researcher found that they spoke about a range of topics, and at first he would only make notes of what he thought was most important. However, as Bogdan and Taylor (1975) advise, even small talk can lend an insight into the subjects' perspectives and may cause a reinterpretation in the observer's understanding of the setting when viewed in context later. This, therefore, prompted the researcher to record as much as possible of the day's events when in the field. Over the duration of the study in 2010-14, a considerable amount of data was obtained on the lives of the young men, and, as Glesne and Peshkin (1992) note, this is to be expected when conducting qualitative studies.

The next task was analysing the data, and organising it in terms of what has been seen, heard, and read so that sense can be made of what is learned (Glesne and Peshkin, 1992). The next section of this chapter discusses data analysis.

Validity of data obtained

One of the foremost risks with the study was with the validity of the data obtained on the lives of the young men. Trochim and Donnelly (2007) define validity as the 'best approximation of the truth'. There was a risk, as there is in most qualitative studies, that actors may deliberately and knowingly attempt to manipulate the impressions they give in order to control the perceptions of the observer. This challenge is understood to be even more the case when studying the lives of those who offend, as the veracity for truth in criminal populations has been questioned with regard to self-reports (Rouse et al, 1985).

In the case of studying the lives of young British Pakistani Muslim men who offend it was difficult to verify The Boys' statements, so a great deal had to be taken on trust. However, as Morse et al (2002) argue, while trustworthiness and its four criteria (credibility, transferability, dependability and conformability) are important evaluation tools, they are limited to assessing the utility of completed research. In the case of this study then, given that the researcher already knew many of The Boys and had been aware of some of their behaviours, verification was difficult yet possible.

Another way of ensuring validity was through the process of interviewing techniques, which helped ensure consistency of the narratives being told by those under study (Creswell, 2008). Interviews were conducted with each of The Boys, but these were not formal, as we discuss in the next section of this chapter. The researcher was very careful in creating codes to help understand descriptions and meanings, making sense of the essential meanings of the phenomenon, which was to understand the lives of the young men as lived by them. After careful reading of the data obtained, themes were identified and the data was divided into meaningful sections (Kleiman, 2004). Due to the sensitivity of the data obtained, it was documented and typed using a secure computer file. All files and documentation in any given format or importance were subsequently shredded. The Boys needed to have confidence in the researcher if they were to open up in any meaningful sense at all with their thoughts and allow someone else to see their lives. Being committed to the study and its participants, the researcher had an obligation to the individuals who had allowed him to observe, interview and conduct the research about them. This obligation included ensuring that (unless in very exceptional circumstances where ethical considerations take priority) nothing could be traced directly back to them to create further difficulties for them.

Methods used to collate data

There are several ways of collecting data for phenomenological research. The most common method is the unstructured or semi-structured interview (Colaizzi, 1978; Wimpenny and Gass, 2000). From the very outset, the researcher had planned to conduct a combination of in-depth interviews with each of The Boys, aware that empirical phenomenology approaches normally require verbal interaction with those studied in the field, for which interviews are most suitable (Schutz, 1976). Interviews would provide an opportunity to ask The Boys questions about their personal lives and offending behaviour in more depth.

In this case, the target population was not self-reflective, analytical or articulate and, although highly intelligent, in most cases their intelligence was untrained. Questions about their lives asked by people who they felt were unable to understand their lives could cause The Boys distress. This became clear on an occasion when Kamran was running late for his probation appointment and was telling The Boys how much he despised going to see his probation officer: "I've done my stretch [sentence in prison]. Why the fuck do I have to see a probation officer? As if it's gonna change my life around now by going to see someone sat behind a desk who haven't got a fucking clue what I've been through."

Self-indulgence, self-consciousness, self-criticism and self-awareness were totally alien to The Boys. They lived spontaneously, and enjoyed elements of secrecy, especially from outsiders who came from different ethnic, religious or cultural backgrounds. They were wary of professionals, particularly those such as teachers, social workers, police, probation officers and court officials. As a consequence, it was crucial that the researcher did not present the study to them as another way of monitoring their criminal behaviour, as if he did then their response would be rather blunt, and they would not approve of their lives being studied. The researcher felt that it was paramount that The Boys were not made to feel singled out, and for this reason he never made them feel under a spotlight, sensing that this would help build mutual trust.

It is important to point out that, while researchers are comfortable and familiar with the academic world, for many young men on the streets their norms can mean that the world of academia is alien, and because it is alien, it is also threatening. The only people who have, in their experience, shown interest on previous occasions have tended to be police, courts, social workers, probation officers and so on, and their interest has unfailingly been seen as malign.

The researcher felt that, instead of conducting long interviews, shorter, potentially more insightful and snappier kinds of questions would be more appropriate, providing they were interspersed with other non-threatening conversations and activities. It was, so to speak, like taking a medication where a little and often was far more productive than one prolonged treatment. One way of conducting interviews was to have a number of short interviews (with the first interview lacking any real direction) with general questions being asked, and then in subsequent interviews to begin focusing the questions much more by asking The Boys more about their lives and offending. The idea behind the initial short interviews was to help them to become familiar with the interview process, aimed at trying to establish trust and a process of opening up, to be followed by further interviews over the following days or weeks. It was anticipated that in the later interviews participants would speak more openly and profoundly with less caution and more honesty than in the early stages as a result of increased trust between interviewee and interviewer. This was based on Sjöberg, Brymer and Farris's (1966: 306) advice to:

> establish long term relationships with respondents, rather than to conduct single or multiple interviews. As the acquaintance process develops the researcher has to be viewed as a 'good guy', an 'insider', and gain access to certain kinds of information that are not otherwise available.

As most of the young men involved in the research have grown to be suspicious of anyone asking questions of any sort about their personal lives, they felt uneasy with the entire process of structured interviews. The researcher had planned from the outset to use a voice recorder in the interviews, as he felt that it would be more suitable than him making notes as The Boys spoke. However, he quickly learned that asking participants to open up with articulate self-analysis in the presence of a voice recorder was simply unrealistic. Recording the interviewees proved to intensify mistrust, even when the researcher was known to the participants. The participants did not completely believe assurances that the tape was for research purposes only, fearing that it may be used by the police (or some other hostile agent) against the person whose comments were being recorded. In one of the earlier interviews conducted after a few months in the field, the researcher recognised that the presence of the voice recorder left The Boys feeling extremely edgy, to the point that the participant being interviewed was reluctant to speak when the recording device was on. The researcher was forced to stop recording, and had to take out the batteries in order to convince the study's participant that the interview was no longer being recorded. Therefore, it became necessary simply to discuss (within extreme limits) the experiences of the respondents and, as far as they were able to articulate them, their understanding of their situations, without making notes or recording such discussions. This intensified the urgent need of writing up all the information as soon as possible afterwards: any delay between holding in the mind any conversation and writing it up later increased the risks of lapse of memory.

The researcher had initially planned to conduct the interviews in restaurants or in fast-food outlets, as these were places The Boys frequented the most and where they felt comfortable. However, in the one interview that did take place in a fast-food outlet, the individual being interviewed was incredibly cautious of whether anyone at the restaurant was looking at him strangely, or if anyone was able to hear the conversation we were having.

As a result of these difficulties, the idea of sitting down and interviewing any of The Boys was scrapped. Instead, whenever the opportunity came about the researcher would speak with individual participants. The researcher sought opportunities where he was able to talk with the participants on their own, being aware that there was rarely a time when any of The Boys were on their own. One characteristic that emerged early on in the research was the realisation that the participants of the study were very aware of each other's presence. The Boys adapted their own behaviour to take into account how they felt the others would respond to their comments. There were times when it was more appropriate to speak individually with respondents in a setting where they would feel relaxed, for example in a gymnasium or at Bash's flat. In a car was a good place for the participants to feel less pressured when answering without thought of other people judging either them or their answers. This scenario was expedient and more apt for the gathering of genuine reflections of their own emotions. The Boys were unaccustomed to 'navel-gazing', and the idea of someone showing interest in their lives was not only unfamiliar but threatening. The idea that they should show a level of sophisticated awareness of their own psyches, their emotions, autobiographies and relationships within the microcosms of the local community and the macro-sociological concerns of wider society was complex, and almost impossible for them to respond to.

Ethical concerns when studying the lives of The Boys in a tight-knit Pakistani community

The study was conducted in an area made up of a number of tightly-knit Pakistani communities, and the nature of the topic raised ethical considerations for the community in which The Boys lived. The researcher had, therefore, to take into account ethical concerns that came with conducting a phenomenological study of the lives of young Pakistani Muslim men who were involved in crime and who lived in a particular area.

One ethical issue was the question whether the present research would leave a negative impact on the community. Would it portray the area and its inhabitants, in particular young men from Pakistani ethnicity, as more criminalised? This variation is perhaps a less-expected concern of the ethics of phenomenology: by using a targeted population who currently reside in a deprived and stigmatised area of Bradford, is the researcher aggravating the scale of deprivation and stigmatisation by publicising negative images of the place and people there? Clearly the concerns of the community had to be considered. Noaks and Wincup (2004: 41) explain:

> Researchers may also encounter ethical issues at a community level. Residents can become concerned about representations of their community, as experiencing significant crime and disorder, and a consequent targeting of their area as a site for research. Residents can have understandable concerns about how the image of their area is negatively affected by subsequent research attention.

In addition, Fisher and Masty (2006: 32) advise: 'When considering the risk benefit ratio for adolescent risk research, especially in minority populations, researchers must be willing to engage in an honest dialogue with participants about the potential positive and negative effects a research study presents from the target community's cultural perspective'.

An effective way to overcome these concerns is to engage the community in the study as partners in the design, as implementation of research can enhance the understanding of the risks, benefits, and fairness of research procedures and increase the probability of community support and cooperation (Thomas and O'Kane, 1998; Sharp and Foster, 2002; Potvin et al, 2003). However, engaging the community in a study which examined the lives and behaviours of young Pakistani Muslim men who were involved in crime could become problematical. First, this would break the confidentiality of the young men, and could make it more difficult to convince them to participate in the study. Second, the concerns of The Boys, who were second- and third-generation Pakistanis, may not correspond with those of the wider community. Fisher and Masty (2006: 24) relevantly state that 'a potential limitation of community consultation is that the concerns and values of community advocates may not reflect the views of the guardians, and adolescents who will actually be recruited to participate in the research'.

This research obviated this potential limitation by conducting initial consultations about the study with the two participants, Kamran and Salman. Although by speaking to and associating with The Boys there was a risk of being pulled into their world of criminality, without speaking to them in a way that inspired their confidence, it would have been impossible to gain any insight into their own perception of issues.

A further ethical issue associated with consulting the community was that if someone was known or suspected to be involved in criminal activities, then there was a risk of this affecting family status [*Izzat*] in the community – that is, the risk of the entire family being associated with crime and/or drug dealing in the eyes of the wider community. Therefore, the study needed to be as discreet as possible, without highlighting the extent of The Boys' criminality to others living in the neighbourhood. Another issue is that no one from the community who had had their property vandalised or their car stolen would be happy to know that such behaviour had been known about and yet went unreported. Similarly, no law-abiding parent would be happy to think that it was known that their son had sold drugs or become involved in the purchasing or supplying of drugs. The ethical ramifications of this research were highly problematic and indeed immensely burdensome for the researcher.

Bibliography

Abrams, LS, 2015, Ethical issues in conducting prison-based ethnography, paper presented at Society for Social Work Research, 19th Annual Conference, New Orleans, LA, 16 January

Adler, PA, 1985, *Wheeling and Dealing*, New York: Columbia University Press

Adler, PA, 1993, *Wheeling and Dealing: An Ethnography of an Upper-Level Drug Dealing and Smuggling Community* (2nd edn), New York: Columbia University Press

Ahmed, F, 2014, British Muslims' relationship crisis: marriage, divorce and the role of secular and religious support services, dissertation, University of Bristol

Ahmed, M, 2001, Muslim religious provision in HM Prison Service, *Prison Service Journal*, 137, 19-21

Akers, RL, 1998, *Social Learning and Social Structure: A General Theory of Crime and Deviance*, Boston, MA: Northeastern University Press

Alam, F, 2006, Language and identity in 'Glaswasian' adolescents: an ethnographic and sociolinguistic study of multilingual Muslim girls in an urban secondary school, unpublished Master's thesis, Department of English Language, University of Glasgow

Alam, MY (ed.) 2006, *Made in Bradford*, Pontefract: Route

Alam, MY and Husband, C, 2006, *British-Pakistani Men from Bradford: Linking Narratives to Policy*, York: Joseph Rowntree Foundation

Alexander, C, 2000, *The Asian Gang, Ethnicity, Identity, Masculinity*, Oxford and New York: Berg

Alexander, C, 2004, Imagining the Asian gang: ethnicity, masculinity and youth after 'the riots', *Critical Social Policy*, 24, 4, 526-549, available at: https://doi.org/10.1177/0261018304046675

Allen, C, 2010, *Islamophobia*, Farnham: Ashgate

Allen, S and Barrett, J, 1996, *The Bradford Commission Report* (the Bradford Congress), London: HMSO

Ammar, NH, Weaver, RR and Saxon, S, 2004, Muslims in prison: a case study from Ohio state prisons, *International Journal of Offender Therapy and Comparative Criminology*, 48, 4, 414-28

Anderson, E, 1994, The code of the streets, *The Atlantic Monthly*, 273, 81-94

Anderson, E, 1999, *Code of the Street: Decency, Violence and the Moral Life of the Inner City*, New York: WW Norton

Antonsich, M, 2014, Living together in diversity: a journey from scholarly views to people's voices and back, *Bollettino della Società Geografica Italiana*, 13, 7, 317-37

Anwar, SY and Hussain, RJ, 2013–2014, *The grassroots voices of British-Pakistanis*, available at: http://jawaab.org.uk/wp-content/uploads/2014/10/Jawaab-The-Grassroots-Voices-of-British-Pakistanis-report.pdf

Archer, L, 2001, Muslim brothers, black lads, traditional Asians: British Muslim young men's constructions of 'race', religion and masculinity, *Feminism and Psychology*, 11, 1, 79-105

Archer, L, 2003, *Race, Masculinity and Schooling: Muslim Boys and Education*, Maidenhead: Open University Press

Armstrong, C, 2012, One in five people in district now of Pakistani origin, *Telegraph and Argus*, 12 December, available at: www.thetelegraphandargus.co.uk/news/local/localbrad/10101667.One_in_five_people_in_district_now_of_Pakistani_origin/

Aspers, P, 2009, Empirical phenomenology: a qualitative research approach (The Cologne Seminars), *Indo-Pacific Journal of Phenomenology*, 9, 2, available at: www.ipjp.org/online-issues/send/36-edition-2-october-2009/157-patrikaspers9e2

Babb, P, Butcher. H, Church, J and Zealey, L, 2006, Households and families, *Social Trends*, 36, Office for National Statistics, available at: file:///C:/Users/jm16502/Chrome%20Local%20Downloads/social_trends_36_tcm77-146799.pdf

Bagguley, P and Hussain, Y, 2003, The Bradford 'riot' of 2001: a preliminary analysis, Department of Sociology and Social Policy, University of Leeds, paper presented to the Ninth Alternative Futures and Popular Protest Conference, Manchester Metropolitan University, 22-24 April

Baker, P, 2010, Representations of Islam in British broadsheet and tabloid newspapers 1999-2005, *Language and Politics*, 9, 2, 310-38

Bari, MA, 2014, Soaring Muslim prison population is a blight on the community, HuffPost, 14 June, available at: http://www.huffingtonpost.co.uk/muhammad-abdul-bari/soaring-muslim-prison-pop_b_5145342.html

Barn, R, 2011, Care leavers and social capital: understanding and negotiating racial and ethnic identity, in T Reynolds (ed.) *Young People, Social Capital and Ethnic Identity*, Abingdon: Routledge, 85-102

Basit, TN, 1997a, *Eastern Values, Western Milieu: Identities and Aspirations of Adolescent British Muslim Girls*, Aldershot: Ashgate

Basit, TN, 1997b, 'I want more freedom, but not too much': British Muslim girls and the dynamism of family values, *Gender and Education*, 9, 4, 425-40

BBC News, 2006, Crime 'hotspot' study angers city, 23 May, available at: http://news.bbc.co.uk/1/hi/uk/5006852.stm

BBC News, 2011, Bradford still 'deeply segregated' after riot in 2001, 7 July, available at: http://www.bbc.co.uk/news/uk-england-leeds-14063086

BBC News, 2015, Fox apology for Birmingham 'Muslim-only' city claim, 18 January, available at: http://www.bbc.co.uk/news/uk-england-birmingham-30870062

BBC News, 2017, Rotherham grooming: woman abused as a child goes public, 20 March, available at: http://www.bbc.co.uk/news/uk-england-south-yorkshire-39291869

Becker, HS, 1963, *Outsiders: Studies in the Sociology of Deviance*, New York: Macmillan

Benson, S, 1996, Asians have culture, West Indians have problems, in T Ranger, Y Samad and O Stuart (eds) *Culture, Identity and Politics*, Aldershot: Avebury Press, 47–56.

Berk, R and Adams, J, 1970, Establishing rapport with deviant groups, *Social Problems*, 18, 1, 102-17

Bhui, HS, 2009, Prisons and race equality, in HS Bhui (ed.) *Race and Criminal Justice*, London: Sage, 83-102

Bhui, HS (ed.) 2010, *Muslim Prisoners' Experiences: A Thematic Review*, London: HM Chief Inspector of Prisons

Blumstein, A and Cohen, J, 1987, Characterizing criminal careers, *Science*, 237, 4818, 985-91

Bogdan, R and Taylor, SJ, 1975, *Introduction to Qualitative Research Methods: A Phenomenological Approach to the Social Sciences*, New York: Wiley

Bolognani, M, 2009, *Crime and Muslim Britain; Race, Culture and the Politics of Criminology Among British Pakistanis*, London: IB Tauris

Bourgois, P, 2003, *In Search of Respect: Selling Crack in El Barrio*, New York: Cambridge University Press

Boys, A, Marsden, J and Strang, J, 2001, Understanding reasons for drug use amongst young people: a functional perspective, *Health Education Research*, 16, 4, 457-469

Bradby, H, 2007, Watch out for the aunties! Young British Asians' accounts of identity and substance use, *Sociology of Health and Illness*, 29, 5, 656-72

Bryman, A, 2004, *Social Research Methods* (2nd edn), Oxford: Oxford University Press

Bucerius, SM, 2014, *Unwanted: Muslim immigrants, dignity, and drug dealing*, New York: Oxford University Press

Bukstel, LH and Kilmann, PR, 1980, Psychological effects of imprisonment on confined individuals, *Psychological Bulletin*, 88, 2, 469-93

Burgess, RL and Akers, RL, 1968, A differential association reinforcement theory of criminal behaviour, *Social Problems*, 14, 2, 128-47

Burke, RD, 2008, *Young People, Crime and Justice*, Cullompton: Willan

Burke, RD, 2009, *An Introduction to Criminological Theory*, Cullompton: Willan

Burnett, R and Farrell, G, 1994, *Reported and Unreported Racial Incidents in Prisons*, Oxford: Centre for Criminological Research, University of Oxford

Burnhill, P, Garner, C and McPherson, A, 1990, Parental education, social class and entry into higher education 1976-86, *Journal of the Royal Statistical Society Series A*, 153, 233-48

Butler, M, 2008, What are you looking at? Prisoner confrontations and the search for respect, *British Journal of Criminology*, 48, 6, 856-73

Carter, H, 2002, '£1m a day' drug road damned by judge, *The Guardian*, 16 September, available at: https://www.theguardian.com/society/2002/sep/16/drugsandalcohol.drugs

Case, S, Johnson, P, Manlow, D, Smith, R and Williams, K, 2017, *Criminology*, Oxford: Oxford University Press, 277

Census, 2011, Ethnicity and national identity in England and Wales 2011 coverage: England and Wales, Date: 11 December 2012: Geographical area: Local authority and county theme: People and places, available at: http://webarchive.nationalarchives.gov.uk/20160107112033/http://www.ons.gov.uk/ons/dcp171776_290558.pdf

Chakraborti, N, 2007, Policing Muslim Communities, in M Rowe (ed.) *Policing Beyond Macpherson: Issues in Policing, Race and Society*, Cullompton: Willan, 107-27

Change Institute, The, Department for Communities and Local Government, 2009, The Pakistani Muslim community in England: Understanding Muslim ethnic communities, March, available at: http://webarchive.nationalarchives.gov.uk/20120920001118/http://www.communities.gov.uk/documents/communities/pdf/1170952.pdf

Chu, CM, Daffern, M, Thomas, SDM and Lim, JY, 2012, Violence risk and gang affiliation in youth offenders: A recidivism study, *Psychology, Crime & Law*, 18, 299-315

Cockbain, E, 2013, Grooming and the 'Asian sex gang predator': The construction of a racial crime threat, *Race and Class*, 54, 4, 22-32

Cockburn, P, 2014, Who are Isis? The rise of the Islamic State in Iraq and the Levant: The group, led since 2010 by Abu Bakr al-Baghdadi, now controls vast swathes of land across Iraq and Syria, *The Independent*, 16 June, available at: http://www.independent.co.uk/news/world/middle-east/who-are-isis-the-rise-of-the-islamic-state-in-iraq-and-the-levant-9541421.html

Cohen, AK, 1955, *Delinquent Boys: The Culture of the Gang*, New York: The Free Press

Cohen, S, 1972, *Folk Devils and Moral Panics*, London: MacGibbon and Kee

Cohen, S and Taylor, L, 1972, *Psychological Survival*, Harmondsworth: Penguin

Colaizzi, PF, 1978, Psychological research as the phenomenologist views it, in RS Valle and M King (eds) *Existential Phenomenological Alternatives for Psychology*, New York: Oxford University Press, 48-71

Conroy, SA, 2003, A pathway for interpretive phenomenology, *International Journal of Qualitative Methods*, 2, 3, 1-43

Cook, F and Wilkinson, M, 1998, *Hard cell*, Liverpool: The Bluecoat Press

Cressey, GR, 2002, Followers of tradition, products of hybridity, or bearers of change? British Pakistani and Kashmiri young people, *Sociale Wetenschappen* [*Social Sciences*], 45, 2, 44-60

Creswell, JW, 2008, *Educational Research: Planning, Conducting, and Evaluating Quantitative and Qualitative Research* (3rd edn), Upper Saddle River, NJ: Parson Merrill Prentice Hall

Crewe, B, 2009, *The Prisoner Society: Power, Adaptation and Social Life in an English Prison*, Oxford: Oxford University Press

Croall, H, 2011, *Crime and Society in Britain* (2nd edn), Harlow: Pearson Education

Curran, DJ and Renzetti, CM (eds) 1994, *Contemporary Societies: Problems and Prospects*, Englewood Cliffs, NJ: Prentice Hall

Currie, T, 2009, *Left hooks and dangerous crooks*, Clacton on Sea: Apex Publishing Ltd

Cusson, M, 1983, *Why Delinquency?* Toronto: University of Toronto Press

Dahya, B, 1974, 'The nature of Pakistani ethnicity in industrial cities in Britain', in A Cohen (ed.) *Urban Ethnicity*, London: Tavistock, 77-118

Denham, J, 2002, Building cohesive communities: A report of the ministerial group on public order and community cohesion, available at: http://www.tedcantle.co.uk/publications/005%20Building%20 Cohesive%20Communities%20%28The%20Denham%20 Report%29%202001.pdf

Din, I, 2006, *The New British: The Impact of Culture and Community on Young Pakistanis*, Aldershot: Ashgate

Dobbs, J, Green, H and Zealey, L (eds) 2006, *Focus on ethnicity and religion*, Basingstoke: Palgrave Macmillan

Dorling, D and Rees, P, 2003, A nation dividing? Some interpretations of the question, *Environment and Planning A*, 36, 2, 369-73

Elliott, DS, 1962, Delinquency and perceived opportunity, *Sociological Inquiry*, 32, 2, 216-227

Emler, N and Reicher, S, 1995, *Adolescence and delinquency: The collective management of reputation*, Cambridge, MA: Blackwell

Fagan, J and Wilkinson, DL, 1998, Guns, violence and social identity in inner cities, in M Tonry and MH Moore (eds) *Youth Violence: Crime and Justice Volume 24*, Chicago, IL: University of Chicago Press, 105-88

Farrington, DP, 1978, The family backgrounds of aggressive youths, in LA Hersov, M Berger and D Shaffer (eds) *Aggression and Antisocial Behaviour in Childhood and Adolescence*, Oxford: Pergamon, 73-93

Farrington, DP, 1997, Human development and criminal careers, in M Maguire, R Morgan and R Reiner (eds) *The Oxford Handbook of Criminology* (2nd edn), Oxford: Clarendon Press, 511-84

Farrington, DP, 2002, Risk factors for youth violence, in É Debarbieux and C Blaya (eds) *Violence in Schools and Public Policies*, Oxford: Elsevier Science, 13-32

Ferrell, J, Hayward, K and Young, J, 2008, *Cultural Criminology*, London: Sage

Fetterman, DM, 1998, *Ethnography: Step by Step* (2nd edn), Applied Social Research Methods Series, Volume 17, Thousand Oaks, CA: Sage

Fisher, C and Masty, J, 2006, Through the community looking glass: participant consultation for adolescent risk research, in B Leadbeater, E Banister, C Benoit, M Jansson, A Marshall and T Riecken (eds) *Ethical Issues in Community-Based Research With Children and Youth*, Toronto: University of Toronto Press, 22-41

Genders, E and Player, E, 1989, *Race Relations in Prisons*, Oxford: Clarendon Press

Gill, AK and Harrison, K, 2015, Child grooming and sexual exploitation: are South Asian men the UK media's new folk devils? *International Journal for Crime Justice and Social Democracy*, 4, 2, 34-49

Gillborn, D, 2002, *Education and Institutional Racism*, London: Institute of Education, University of London

Giordano, PC, Cernkovich, SA and Pugh, MD, 1986, Friendships and delinquency, *American Journal of Sociology*, 91, 5, 1170–1202

Glaser, D, 1960, Differential association and criminological prediction, *Social Problems*, 8, 1, 6-14

Glesne, C and Peshkin, A, 1992, *Becoming Qualitative Researchers: An Introduction*, White Plains, NY: Longman

Goodey, J, 1998, Examining the 'white racist/black victim' stereotype, *International Review of Victimology*, 5, 3/4, 235-56

Goodey, J, 2001, The criminalization of British Asian youth: research from Bradford and Sheffield, *Journal of Youth Studies*, 4, 4, 429-50

Graham, J and Bowling, B, 1995, *Young People and Crime*, Home Office Research Study 145, London: Home Office

Greig, A and Taylor, J, 1999, *Doing Research With Children*, London: Sage

Grund, TU and Densley, JA, 2012, Ethnic heterogeneity in the activity and structure of a Black street gang, *European Journal of Criminology*, 9, 4, 388-406

Guardian, The, 2001, 'Systemic failures' led to racist prison murder, 5 October, available at: https://www.theguardian.com/uk/2001/oct/05/race.world

Hall, A, 2013, *The story of Bradford*, Stroud: The History Press

Hall, S, 1978, *Policing the Crisis: Mugging, the State and Law and Order*, London: Macmillan

Hamm, MS, 2009, Prison Islam in the age of sacred terror, *British Journal of Criminology*, 49, 5, 667-85

Hargreaves, J, 2014, Half a story? Missing perspectives in the criminological accounts of British Muslim communities, crime and the criminal justice system, *British Journal of Criminology*, 55, 1, 19-33

Harrington, R and Bailey, S, 2005, *Mental health needs and effectiveness provision for young offenders in custody and in the community*, London: Youth Justice Board

Hay, B, 2005, Sting operations, undercover agents, and entrapment, *Missouri Law Review*, 70, 2

Hayden, C, Williamson, T and Webber, R, 2006, Schools, pupil behaviour and young offenders, *British Journal of Criminology*, 47, 2, 293-310

Hillyard, P, 1993, *Suspect Community: People's Experiences of the Prevention of Terrorism Acts in Britain*, London: Pluto Press

Hirschi, T, 2002, *Causes of Delinquency*, New Brunswick, NJ: Transaction Publishers

Hoffer, LD, 2006, *Junkie Business: The Evolution and Operation of a Heroin Dealing Network*, Belmont, CA: Thompson Wadsworth

Holloway, I, 1997, *Basic Concepts for Qualitative Research*, Oxford: Blackwell Science

Hopkins Burke, RD, 1999, *Youth, Justice and the Fragmentation of Modernity*, Occasional Paper Series, Leicester: Scarman Centre for the Study of Public Order

Horabin, R, 1978, *Problems of Asians in Penal Institutions*, London: Runnymede Trust and The Howard League for Penal Reform

House of Commons Home Affairs Committee, 2015, *Roots of violent radicalisation*, Nineteenth Report of Session 2010–12, Volume I: Report, together with formal minutes, oral and written evidence. Additional written evidence contained in Volume II, available at: www.parliament.uk/homeaffairscom

Hudson, B, 2007, Diversity, crime and criminal justice, in M Maguire, R Morgan and R Reiner (eds) *The Oxford Handbook of Criminology* (4th edn), Oxford: Oxford University Press, 158-71

Hudson, M, Davidson, R, Durante, L, Grieve, J and Kazmi, A, 2011, *Recession and Cohesion in Bradford*, York: Joseph Rowntree Foundation

Hussain Y and Bagguley P, 2009, The Bradford 'riot' of 2001: The diversity of action, in D Waddington, F Jobard and M King (eds) *Rioting in the UK and France: A comparative analysis*, Cullompton: Willan, 71-80

Inman, P, 2014, Minority ethnic workers in UK twice as likely to be unemployed as whites: DWP figures show jobless rate of 45% for young black, Pakistani and Bangladeshi workers with white figure at 19%, *The Guardian*, 8 January, available at: https://www.theguardian.com/society/2014/jan/08/minority-ethnic-workers-more-often-unemployed

Jacobs, BA, 1996, Crack dealers and restrictive deterrence: identifying narcs, *Criminology*, 34, 3, 409-31

Jacobs, BA, 1999, *Dealing Crack: The Social World of Streetcorner Selling*, Boston, MA: Northeastern University Press

Jamieson, R and Grounds, AT, 2005, Release and adjustment: perspectives from studies of wrongly convicted and politically motivated prisoners, in A Liebling and S Maruna (eds) *The Effects of Imprisonment*, Cullompton: Willan, 33-65

Jewkes, Y, 2002, *Captive Audience: Media, Masculinity and Power in Prisons*, Cullompton: Willan

Jewkes, Y, 2005, Loss, liminality and the life sentence, in A Liebling and S. Maruna (eds) *The Effects of Imprisonment*, Cullompton: Willan, 366-88

Johnson, BD and Natarajan, M, 1995, Strategies to avoid arrest: crack sellers' response to intensified policing, *American Journal of Police*, 14, 3/4, 49-69

Johnson, J, 1975, *Doing Field Research*, New York: Free Press

Jones, C, 1993, Auditing criminal justice, *British Journal of Criminology*, 33, 3, 187-202

Joseph Rowntree Foundation, 2007, *Poverty rates among ethnic groups in Great Britain*, York: Joseph Rowntree Foundation

Joseph Rowntree Foundation, 2011, *Recession, poverty and sustainable livelihoods in Bradford*, York: Joseph Rowntree Foundation

Kalra, V, 2003, Police lore and community disorder: diversity in the criminal justice system, in D Mason (ed.) *Explaining Ethnic Differences: Changing Patterns of Disadvantage in Britain*, Bristol: Policy Press

Karpa, DR, 2010, Unlocking men, unmasking masculinities: Doing men's work in prison, *The Journal of Men's Studies*, 18, 1

Katz, J, 1988, *Seductions of Crime: Moral and Sensual Attractions of Doing Evil*, New York: Basic Books

King, WR, 2000, Measuring police innovation: issues and measurement, *Policing: An International Journal of Police Strategies and Management*, 23, 3, 303-17

Kitzmann, KM, Gaylord, NK, Holt, AR and Kenny, ED, 2003, Child witnesses to domestic violence: a meta-analytic review, *Journal of Consulting and Clinical Psychology*, 71, 2, 339-52

Kleiman, S, 2004, Phenomenology: to wonder and search for meanings, *Nurse Researcher*, 11, 4, 7-19

Koenig, HG, 1995, Religion and older men in prison, *International Journal of Geriatric Psychology*, 10, 3, 219-30

Kubrin, CE, 2005, Gangstas, thugs, and hustlas: identity and the code of the street in rap music, *Social Problems*, 52, 3, 360-78

Kundnani, A, 2006, Racial profiling and anti-terror stop and search, *Institute of Race Relations*, available at: www.irr.org.uk/news/racial-profiling-and-anti-terror-stop-and-search/

Lampert, MD and Ervin-Tripp, SM, 2006, Risky laughter: teasing and self-directed joking among male and female friends, *Journal of Pragmatics*, 38, 1, 51-72

Lewis, P, 1994, *Islamic Britain: Religion, Politics and Identity Among British Muslims*, London: IB Taurus

Liebling, A and Maruna, S (eds) 2005, *The Effects of Imprisonment*, Cullompton: Willan

Loweth, J, 2013, Concerns over 'social norm' drug dealing in Bradford, *Telegraph and Argus*, 3 September, available at: www.thetelegraphandargus.co.uk/news/10649418.Concerns_over____social_norm____drug_dealing_in_Bradford/

Macey, M, 1999, Class, gender and religious influences on changing patterns of Pakistani Muslim male violence in Bradford, *Ethnic and Racial Studies*, 22, 5, 845-66

Macey, M, 2002, 'Interpreting Islam: young Muslim men's involvement in criminal activity in Bradford', in B Spalek (ed.) *Islam, Crime and Criminal Justice*, Cullompton: Willan

Maguire, M, 2000, Researching 'street criminals' in the field: a neglected art?, in RD King and E Wincup (eds) *Doing Research on Crime and Justice*, Oxford: Oxford University Press

Maguire, M, Morgan, R and Reiner, R, 2007, *The Oxford Handbook of Criminology* (4th edn), Oxford: Oxford University Press

Marsh, I, 2006, *Theories of Crime*, Abingdon: Routledge

Martin, C, 2000, Doing research in a prison setting, in V Jupp, P Davies and P Francis (eds) *Doing Criminological Research*, Thousand Oaks, CA: Sage, 215-33

Maruna, S, Wilson, L and Curran, K, 2006, Why God is often found behind bars: prison conversions and the crisis of self-narrative, *Research in Human Development*, 3, 2&3, 161–184

Mawby, RI and Batta, ID, 1980, *Asians and Crime: The Bradford Experience*, London: Scope Communications

May, T and Hough, M, 2004, Drug markets and distribution systems, *Addiction Research & Theory*, 12, 6, 549-63

McGivern, MS, 2010, The impact of cognitive coping on the strain-delinquency relationship: a test of general strain theory, Master's thesis, University of Iowa, available at: http://ir.uiowa.edu/etd/550

Merton, RK, 1968, Social structure and anomie, in RK Merton, *Social Theory and Social Structure* (enlarged edn), New York: The Free Press, 185-214

Miller, W, 1958, Lower class culture as a generating milieu of gang delinquency, *Journal of Social Issues*, 14, 3, 5-19

Miner-Romanoff, K, 2012, Interpretive and critical phenomenological crime studies: a model design, *The Qualitative Report*, 17, 27, 1-32

Modood, T (ed.) 1997, *Church, State and Religious Minorities*, London: Policy Studies Institute

Modood, T, Hoffman, S and Virdee, S, 1994, *Changing Ethnic Identities*, London: Policy Studies Institute

MORI (Market and Opinion Research International) 2004, *MORI Youth Survey 2004*, London: Youth Justice Board

Morse, J, Barrett, M, Mayan, M, Olson, K and Spiers, J, 2002, Verification strategies for establishing reliability and validity in qualitative research, *International Journal of Qualitative Methods*, 1, 2, 1-19

Myers, D, Milne, A, Baker, K. and Ginsburg, A, 1987, Student discipline and high school performance, *Sociology of Education*, 60, 18-33

Mythen, G, Walklate, S and Khan, F, 2009, 'I'm a Muslim, but I'm not a terrorist': victimization, risky identities and the performance of safety, *British Journal of Criminology*, 49, 6, 736-54

Noaks, L and Wincup, E, 2004, *Criminological Research: Understanding Qualitative Methods*, London: Sage

Oake, S, 2012, The eccentric benefactor, *Dalesman*, April, 70-3

Office for National Statistics, 2015, Release edition reference tables, 25 June

Orford, J, Johnson, M and Purser, B, 2004, Drinking in second generation Black and Asian communities in the English midlands, *Addiction Research & Theory*, 12, 1, 11-30

Pager, D, 2003, The mark of a criminal record, *American Journal of Sociology*, 108, 5, 937-75

Pantazis, C and Pemberton, S, 2009, From the 'old' to the 'new' suspect community examining the impacts of recent UK counter-terrorist legislation, *British Journal of Criminology*, 49, 5, 646-66

Pargeter, A, 2006, North African immigrants in Europe and political violence, *Studies in Conflict and Terrorism*, 29, 7, 731-47

Parker, H, 1974, *View from the Boys: A sociology of down-town adolescents*, Newton Abbot: David and Charles, pp. 234

Parker, H, Bakx, K and Newcombe, R, 1988, *Living with Heroin: The Impact of a Drugs 'Epidemic' on an English Community*, Milton Keynes: Open University Press

Patel, TG and Tyrer, D, 2011, *Race, Crime and Resistance*, London: Sage

Patrick, J, 1973, *A Glasgow Gang Observed*, London: Eyre Methuen

Pearce J and Bujra J, 2006, Young men without a future who brought terror to a city, *Yorkshire Post*, 1 July

Pearson, A, 2012, Asian sex gang: Young girls betrayed by our fear of racism, *The Telegraph*, 9 May, available at http://www.telegraph.co.uk/news/uknews/crime/9254651/Asian-sexgang-young-girls-betrayed-by-our-fear-of-racism.html

Pearson, G, 2001, Drugs and poverty, in S Chen and E Skidelsky (eds) *High Time for Reform: Drug Policy for the 21st Century*, London: Social Market Foundation

Phillips, C, 2003, Who's who in the pecking order? Aggression and 'normal violence' in the lives of girls and boys, *British Journal of Criminology*, 43, 4, 710-28

Phillips, C and Brown, D, 1998, *Entry Into the Criminal Justice System: A Survey of Police Arrests and Their Outcomes*, Home Office Research Study 185, London: Home Office

Phillips, D, 2002, *Movement to Opportunity? South Asian Relocation in Northern Cities*, End of Award report, ESRC R000238038, Leeds: School of Geography, University of Leeds

Polsky, N, 1969, *Hustlers, Beats and Others*, Harmondsworth: Penguin

Poole, E and Richardson, JE (eds) 2006, *Muslims and the News Media*, London: IB Tauris

Potvin, L, Cargo, M, McComber, AM, Delormier, T and Macaulay, AC, 2003, Implementing participatory intervention and research in communities: lessons from the Kahnawake Schools Diabetes Prevention Project, *Social Science & Medicine*, 56, 6, 1295-305

Powell, JL and Wahidin, A, 2009, *Risk and Social Welfare*, New York: Nova

Poynting, S and Mason, V, 2006, 'Tolerance, freedom, justice and peace'? Britain, Australia and anti–Muslim racism since 11 September 2001, *Journal of Intercultural Studies*, 27, 4, 365-91

Poynting, S and Mason, V, 2007, The resistible rise of Islamophobia: anti-Muslim racism in the UK and Australia before 11 September 2001, *Journal of Sociology*, 43, 1, 61-86

Pring, R, 1996, Educating persons: putting 'education' back into educational research, *Scottish Educational Review*, 27, 2, 101-12

Qasim, M, 2017, Explaining young British Muslim men's involvement in heroin and crack, *Criminology and Criminal Justice,* first published 9 April, available at: https://doi.org/10.1177/1748895817704024

Quraishi, M, 2005, *Muslims and Crime: A Comparative Study*, Aldershot: Ashgate

Qureshi, K, Charsley, K and Shaw, A, 2014, Marital instability among British Pakistanis: transnationality, conjugalities and Islam, *Ethnic and Racial Studies*, 37, 2, 261-79

Rahman, S, 2009, Segregation in Bradford, *The Guardian*, 21 December, available at: www.theguardian.com/commentisfree/belief/2009/dec/21/bradford-islam-white-flight-segregation

Reiss, AJ Jr, 1986, Why are communities important in understanding crime? in AJ Reiss Jr and M Tonry (eds) *Communities and Crime*, Chicago, IL: University of Chicago Press, 1-34

Rethink, 2006, Our voice: the Pakistani community's view of mental health and mental health services in Birmingham, report from the Aap Ki Awaaz project, available at: https://lemosandcrane.co.uk/resources/Rethink%20-%20Our%20Voice.pdf

Riaz, U, 2004, *The Experiences of Older Pakistani People in Bradford*, Research on Age Discrimination Research Report 7, Open University

Rivera, RJ and Short, JF Jr, 1967, Significant adults, caretakers, and structures of opportunity: an exploratory study, *Journal of Research in Crime and Delinquency*, 4, 1, 76-97

Rose, N, 1994, Expertise and the government of conduct, *Studies in Law, Politics and Society*, 14, 359-97

Rouse, BA, Kozel, NJ and Richards, LG, 1985, *Self-Report Methods of Estimating Drug Use: Meeting Current Challenges to Validity*, Rockville, MD: National Institute on Drug Abuse

Rowe, M, 2012, *Race and Crime: A Critical Engagement*, London: Sage

Ruggiero V and Khan, K, 2006, British South Asian communities and drug supply networks in the UK, *International Journal of Drug Policy*, 17, 473–83

Runnymede Trust, 1997, *Commission on British Muslims and Islamophobia, Islamophobia: A Challenge to Us All: Report of the Runnymede Trust Commission on British Muslims and Islamophobia*, Runnymede Trust

Rushdie, S, 1989, *The Satanic Verses*, London: Viking

Sampson, RJ, 2010, Gold standard myths: observations on the experimental turn in quantitative criminology, *Journal of Quantitative Criminology*, 26, 4, 489-500

Sampson, RJ and Laub, JH, 1993, *Crime in the Making: Pathways and Turning Points Through Life*, Cambridge, MA: Harvard University Press

Sampson, RJ and Laub, JH, 1995, Understanding variability in lives through time: contributions of life-course criminology, *Studies on Crime and Crime Prevention*, 4, 2, 143-58

Sampson, RJ and Laub, JH, 2003, Desistance from crime over the life course, in JT Mortimer and MJ Shanahan (eds) *Handbook of the Life Course*, New York: Plenum/Kluwer, 295-310

Sandberg, S, 2008, Black drug dealers in a white welfare state: cannabis dealing and street capital in Norway, *British Journal of Criminology*, 48, 5, 604-19

Sandberg, S and Pedersen, W, 2011, *Street capital: Black cannabis dealers in a white welfare state*, Chicago: The University of Chicago Press

Sarnecki, J, 1986, *Delinquent Networks*, Report 1, Stockholm: National Council for Crime Prevention

Saul, H, 2015, Katie Hopkins urged to apologise for dehumanising column comparing refugees to 'cockroaches' after Independent campaign, *The Independent*, 3 September, available at: http://www.independent.co.uk/news/people/katie-hopkins-urged-to-apologise-for-dehumanising-column-comparing-refugees-to-cockroaches-after-10484400.html

Schutz, A, 1962, *Collected Papers I: The Problem of Social Reality*, M Natansan (ed.), The Hague: Martinus Nijhoff

Schutz, A, 1976, *The Phenomenology of the Social World*, London: Heinemann Educational Books

Shackle, S, 2010, The mosques aren't working in Bradistan: Bradford's Pakistani community predominantly originates from the Mirpur region, *New Statesman*, 20 August, available at: http://www.newstatesman.com/society/2010/08/bradford-british-pakistan

Sharp, C, Aldridge, J and Medina, J, 2004, *Delinquent Youth Groups and Offending Behaviour: Findings from the 2004 Offending, Crime and Justice Survey*, Home Office online report 14/06

Sharp, RR and Foster, MW, 2002, Community involvement in the ethical review of genetic research: lessons from American Indian and Alaska Native populations, *Environmental Health Perspectives*, 110, S2, 145-8

Shaw, A, 1988, *A Pakistani Community in Britain*, Oxford: Basil Blackwell

Shaw, A, 1994, The Pakistani community in Oxford, in R Ballard (ed.) *Desh Pardesh: The South Asian Presence in Britain*, London: C Hurst

Shaw, A, 2000, *Kinship and Continuity: Pakistani Families in Britain*, Amsterdam: Harwood

Shaw, CR and McKay, HD, 1969, *Juvenile delinquency and urban areas*, Chicago: The University of Chicago Press

Sherrer, PP, 2008, The socio-cultural dimension affecting youth violence behaviour, Faculty of Social Sciences and Humanity, Mahidol University

Sim, J, 1994, Tougher than the rest? Men in prison, in T Newburn and EA Stanko (eds) *Just Boys Doing Business? Men, Masculinities and Crime*, Abingdon: Routledge

Singh, A-M, 2008, *Policing and Crime Control in Post-Apartheid South Africa*, Aldershot: Ashgate

Singh, J, 1994, *Trends in Defence Expenditure in Asian Strategic Review 1993-94*, New Delhi: Institute for Defence Studies and Analyses

Singh, R, 2002, *The Struggle of Racial Justice: From Community Relations to Community Cohesion: The Story of Bradford, 1950-2002*, Bradford: Bradford Arts, Museums and Libraries Service

Sjöberg, G, Brymer, RA and Farris, B, 1966, Bureaucracy and the lower class, *Sociology and Social Research*, 50, 325-37

Smith, D, 2009, Criminology, contemporary society and race issues, in H. Singh Bhui (ed.) *Race and Criminal Justice*, London: Sage, 30-48

Smith, G, 2009, Citizen oversight of independent police services: bifurcated accountability, regulation creep, and lesson learning, *Regulation & Governance*, 3, 4, 421-42

Soller, B, Jackson, AL and Browning, CR, 2014, Legal cynicism and parental appraisals of adolescent violence, *British Journal of Criminology*, 54, 4, 568-591

Spalek, B, 2002a, Introduction, in B Spalek (ed.) *Islam, Crime and Criminal Justice*, Cullompton: Willan

Spalek, B, 2002b, *Islam, Crime and Criminal Justice*, Cullompton: Willan

Spalek, B, 2008, *Communities, Identities and Crime*, Bristol: Policy Press

Spalek, B and El-Hassan, S, 2007, Muslim converts in prison, *The Howard Journal of Crime and Justice*, 46, 2, 99-114

Spalek, B and Lambert, B, 2007, Muslim communities under surveillance, *Criminal Justice Matters*, 68, 1, 12-13

Spalek, B and Wilson, D, 2002, Racism and religious discrimination in prison: the marginalisation of imams in their work with prisoners, in B. Spalek (ed.) *Islam, Crime and Criminal Justice*, Cullompton: Willan, 96-112

Spencer, D, 2009, Sex offender as homo sacer, *Punishment and Society*, 11, 2, 219-40

Sukhodolsky, DG and Ruchkin, VV, 2004, Association of normative beliefs and anger with aggression and antisocial behavior in Russian male juvenile offenders and high school students, *Journal of Abnormal Child Psychology*, 32, 2, 225–236

Sutherland, EH, 1939, *Principles of Criminology* (3rd edn), Philadelphia, PA: Lippincott

Tan, L and Grace, RC, 2008, Social desirability and sexual offenders: a review, *Sexual Abuse: A Journal of Research and Treatment*, 20, 1, 61-87

Taylor, CS, 1990, Gang imperialism, in CR Huff (ed.) *Gangs in America*, Newbury Park, CA: Sage, 103-15

Taylor, S and Gibson, K, 2010, *Manningham: Character and Diversity in a Bradford Suburb*, Swindon: English Heritage

Taylor, SA, 2009, Engaging and retaining vulnerable youth in a short-term longitudinal qualitative study, *Qualitative Social Work*, 8, 3, 391-408

Telegraph and Argus, 1999, Thousands living in a slum squalor, *Telegraph and Argus*, 2 March, available at: www.thetelegraphandargus. co.uk/news/8067557.Thousands_living_in_slum_squalor/

Tewksbury, RA, 2006, *Behind Bars: Readings on Prison Culture*, Pearson/ Prentice Hall

Thomas, N and O'Kane, C, 1998, The ethics of participatory research with children, *Children and Society*, 12, 5, 336-48

Toch, H, 1992, *Violent Men: An Inquiry into the Psychology of Violence* (revised edn), Washington, DC: American Psychological Association

Topalli, V and Wright, R, 2002, Drug dealers, robbery and retaliation. Vulnerability, deterrence and the contagion of violence, *The British Journal of Criminology*, 42, 2, 337–351

Trivedi, C, 1997, Gang warfare, *Eastern Eye*, 2 May

Trochim, WMK and Donnelley, JP, 2007, *The Research Methods Knowledge Base*, Mason, OH: Thomson Custom

Uhrig, N, 2016, *Black, Asian and Minority Ethnic disproportionality in the Criminal Justice System in England and Wales*, London: Ministry of Justice, available at: www.gov.uk/government/uploads/system/ uploads/attachment_data/file/568680/bame-disproportionality-in-the-cjs.pdf

Valentine, SR, 2005, *Muslims in Bradford, UK*, background paper for COMPAS, University of Oxford

Vaswani, N, 2008, *Persistent Offender Profile: Focus on Bereavement*, Briefing Paper 13, Criminal Justice Social Work Development Centre for Scotland, available at: www.cycj.org.uk/wp-content/ uploads/2014/05/Bereavement-Paper-CJSW-Briefing.pdf

Vaughn, MS and Sapp, AD, 1989, Less than utopian: sex offender treatment in a milieu of power struggles, status positioning, and inmate manipulation in state correctional institutions, *Prison Journal*, 69, 2, 73-89

Vold, GB, Bernard, TJ and Snipes, JB, 2002, *Theoretical Criminology* (5th edn), Oxford: Oxford University Press

Wahidin, A, 2009, *Risk and social welfare*, New York: Nova

Wainwright, M, 1995, Divided loyalties, *The Guardian*, 12 June

Waller, M, 2003, Terrorist recruitment and infiltration in the United States: Prisons and military as an operational base, testimony before the U.S. Senate Committee on the Judiciary, 14 October, available at: www.centerforsecuritypolicy.org/2003/10/14/waller-testimony-on-terrorist-infiltration-2/

Wallman, S, 1986, Ethnicity and the boundary process in context, in J Rex and D Mason (eds) *Theories of Race and Ethnic Relations*, Cambridge: Cambridge University Press, 226-35

Wardak, A, 2000, *Social Control and Deviance: A South Asian Community in Scotland*, Aldershot: Ashgate

Warr, M, 2002, *Companions in Crime: The Social Aspects of Criminal Conduct*, Cambridge: Cambridge University Press

Webster, C, 1996, Local heroes: violent racism, localism and spacism among white and Asian young people, *Youth & Policy*, 53, 15-27

Webster, C, 1997a, The construction of British 'Asian' criminality, *International Journal of the Sociology of Law*, 25, 1, 65-86

Webster, C, 1997b, *Understanding Race and Crime*, Maidenhead: Open University Press

Webster, C, 2007, *Understanding Race and Crime*, Maidenhead: Open University Press

Weller, P, Feldman, A and Purdam, K, 2001, *Religious Discrimination in England and Wales*, Home Office Research Study 220, London: Home Office

Werbner, P, 2004, Theorising complex diasporas: purity and hybridity in the South Asian public sphere in Britain, *Journal of Ethnic and Migration Studies*, 30, 5, 895-911

Wilkinson, DL, 2001, Violent events and social identity: specifying the relationship between respect and masculinity in inner city youth violence, in D Kinney (ed.) *Sociological Studies of Children and Youth, Volume 8*, Bingley: Emerald, 231-65

Willis, P, 1990, *Common Culture: Symbolic Work at Play in the Everyday Cultures of the Young*, Milton Keynes: Open University Press

Wilson, D, 2003, 'Keeping quiet' or 'going nuts': some emerging strategies used by young black people in custody at a time of childhood being re-constructed, *Howard Journal of Crime and Justice*, 42, 5, 411-25

Wimpenny, P and Gass, J, 2000, Interviewing in phenomenology and grounded theory: is there a difference? *Journal of Advanced Nursing*, 31, 6, 1485-92

Winfree, LT, Newbold, G and Tubb, SH, 2002, Prisoner perspectives on inmate culture in New Mexico and New Zealand: a descriptive case study, *Prison Journal*, 82, 2, 213-33

Winlow, S, Hall, S and Treadwell, J, 2017, *The Rise of the Right: The English Defence League and the Transformation of Working-Class Politics*, Bristol: Policy Press

Wolcott, HF, 1995, *The Art of Fieldwork*, London: Sage

Wortley, R, 2002, *Situational Prison Control: Crime Prevention in Correctional Institutions*, Cambridge: Cambridge University Press

Wright, S, 2009, Manningham man shouted racial abuse before attack, *Telegraph and Argus*, 20 August, available at: www.thetelegraphandargus. co.uk/news/4555469.Teenager_gets_five_years_for_race_stabbing/

Yablonsky, L, 1965, *Synanon: The Tunnel Back*, New York, Macmillan

Index